FROM
GRIEF
TO
GRATITUDE

One Soul's Journey

Mary Lynn Miller

ISBN 979-8-89112-841-5 (Paperback)
ISBN 979-8-89112-843-9 (Hardcover)
ISBN 979-8-89112-842-2 (Digital)

Copyright © 2024 Mary Lynn Miller
All rights reserved
First Edition

All rights reserved. No part of this publication may be reproduced, distributed, or transmitted in any form or by any means, including photocopying, recording, or other electronic or mechanical methods without the prior written permission of the publisher. For permission requests, solicit the publisher via the address below.

Covenant Books
11661 Hwy 707
Murrells Inlet, SC 29576
www.covenantbooks.com

I would like to dedicate this book to all the special people whom God carefully placed on my path as I journeyed through life—different people, at different places, and for different reasons. Each one of you is precious, and you know who you are.

Mary Lynn Miller knows the well-worn path from grief to hope and offers here a report of the terrain and a gentle hand to guide us on our own journey. She not only challenges us to face the reality of grief, but she also points to hope each step of the way. With candor and vulnerability, Mary Lynn offers a beautiful map for how to navigate pain and loss and how to come out the other side with a deeper and more profound understanding of God and self.

Rev. Dr. Mark E. Parsons
The Presbyterian Church of Dover

Mary Lynn Miller paints a moving, yet magnificent and panoramic canvas of her life to show how one confronts grief by turning it into an uplifting inspiration to guide us in achieving a joyful life. She vividly demonstrates how the heavy burden of grief can be overcome. A must-read for all of us who experience grief and sudden death in our lives.

William L. Witham Jr.
Veterans Treatment Court Judge, Retired

From Grief to Gratitude: One Soul's Journey was not what I initially thought it would be. I thought I was picking up a book to learn how to deal with one's grief. In actuality, this book is so much more. From that small Pennsylvania town to Texas to Florida to Hawaii to Delaware, I was held captive as I walked through Mary Lynn's life with her. You can't help but celebrate, cry, and become angry right along with her. This book is more than grief. It is courage. Bravery. Humility. Humbled beginnings. Compassion. Sadness. Trust. It is about being positive. Being faithful. And never giving up.

Rolonda Sutton-Greene, LPN, CDP
Delaware Hospice
Volunteer Coordinator/Triage Nurse

From Grief to Gratitude: One Soul's Journey is a must-read for anyone feeling loss of any kind! Mary Lynn's faith, love, and experiences with deep loss are shared in a genuine and thought-provoking way, encouraging us to learn new insights into our own thoughts, feelings, and particularly our choices, through grieving. I was blessed with her insight as I read this book during my mother's illness and again after her recent passing. Mary Lynn's journey is a testament to how God uses all things for his good and in his own time.

Lisa Ehret
President, Ehret Accounting, LLC

Beautifully written journey of love and great losses and the faith, strength, and courage to keep going. Such an example of how God inspires us and uses us for his purposes.

Lois Wentz
Author's sister-in-law

CONTENTS

Introduction ix

Chapter 1: Bowl of Cherries 1
Chapter 2: Independent Thoughts 9
Chapter 3: Leaving Home 22
Chapter 4: Trouble in Paradise 35
Chapter 5: Another Choice 48
Chapter 6: A Death without Grief 58
Chapter 7: Good and Plenty 72
Chapter 8: Hello, Goodbye 81
Chapter 9: Now What? 98
Chapter 10: Transplant and Transform 105
Chapter 11: Unexpected Results 122
Chapter 12: The Aftermath 139
Chapter 13: Cumulative Grief 159
Chapter 14: Don't Ask Why 172
Chapter 15: Signs, Gratitude, and Meaning 180
Chapter 16: My Journey Continues… 186

INTRODUCTION

> When you are in the dark, listen, and God
> will give you a very precious message.
> —Oswald Chambers

My journey through grief was not only the most painful experience of my life, it was also the most transformative. After over forty years in the information technology sector, I had retired to take care of my ill husband. When he died, I felt that I had lost my identity. He no longer needed me. My children were grown and raising their own families. My career was over. Who was I? Within three years, I had also lost my two dearest friends.

Part of my grief was missing the ones who had died. The other part was missing who I once was. I was no longer the most important person in the world to anyone. I was no longer anyone's best friend. The happiest memories of my past became the most painful reminders of my loss; it was joy turned upside down. I lived my days in fearful anticipation of the worst that could happen, followed by the crushing realization that the worst already had happened. My relationships with my husband and my friends had no tomorrow.

The pain was staggering. My mind could not fully comprehend the magnitude of my losses, my heart was filled with sorrow, and I could no longer function normally. Depression and sleepless nights numbed my body.

As I lived through the pain each day, I eventually discovered a kind of inner strength that I never knew existed, a kind of understanding that my mind had never experienced. I came to see that grief is about learning that the strength to overcome the pain is actually embedded in the pain itself. As I trusted God and moved through my suffering, I became stronger and wanted to find meaning for my losses and my grief.

Grief changed me. It helped to sculpt me into someone who appreciates more quickly, understands more deeply, hurts more often, cries more easily, hopes more desperately; and, most importantly, loves more openly.

The journey through grief (and beyond) is a very personal journey, and it is different for everyone. Grief is an inevitable emotion that can't be hurried or ignored or even controlled, but it offers profound lessons. My own journey has been an attempt to get in touch with my soul, to find out who I am and why I am here. Surely, my soul could help me understand why. Why was I now left alone? Why was I suffering so deeply? Why was the healing, if there really was any healing, so painful?

There will come a point, after you have honored your grief, when you will want to stop hurting, when your emptiness will become so encompassing that you will want to reduce your suffering. I believe that our loved ones who are in the spirit world are always trying to contact us. They want us to know they are still with us and very much a part of our lives. Communication with lost loved ones is a language built into our souls; it is a direct connection to God. This communication can only be awakened with an openness to believing that extraordinary events can actually occur during ordinary times.

Sadly, most of us are usually too busy to notice the little (and sometimes not so little) signs that surround us. Due to our social conditioning, we rely primarily on our mind for the interpretation of our reality instead of this sacred communication within our soul that is available to each of us. Until we learn to become *more aware* of what is going on around us (and *within* us), until we learn to be more present in our everyday lives, we will miss very important messages from our deceased loved ones.

I have encountered such messages throughout my journey through grief. Just such a message happened one evening at my kitchen table as I was reading a book where an elderly man was having a conversation with a younger man. He was telling the younger man about his time during the war. The older gentleman was relaxed,

INTRODUCTION

enjoying the conversation, and smoking his pipe. As I was absorbed in their conversation, my kitchen began to fill with the aroma of cherry tobacco. I thought of my father, who had passed away several months before. He was a WWII veteran, and he liked to tell stories about his time in the army. He told his stories to us at our kitchen table, and he always smoked a pipe that was filled with his favorite cherry tobacco! I sat in amazement as the cherry tobacco scent descended upon me, and my memories of his stories came to life. There was no doubt in my mind that the familiar tobacco smell was very real.

Over the years, these messages and signs have conjured up an overwhelming sense of warmth and unconditional love. They have comforted and filled me with a sense of peace, and they have reminded me that we truly are never alone.

This personal and deeply awakening journey has instilled in me an intense desire to share what I have learned. As I began to understand the choices I had made, I found a healing process that gave meaning to my grief, and it offered me this opportunity to use what I learned to help others.

The healing didn't mean that my losses didn't happen; it simply meant that they no longer controlled me. It didn't lessen the connection to the ones I had lost; it just decreased the suffering associated with it.

In order to better understand why grief had affected me so deeply, I needed to take a closer look at my life, and the events that shaped it. I needed to understand how my relationships and experiences had affected my decisions, and I had to see more clearly how those choices had molded me into the person I had become.

Each chapter in this book consists of three parts. The first part describes the events during a specific period in my life. The second part is a summary and current-day reflection of those events and how I chose to respond to them. The third part contains three thought-provoking questions. I hope these questions will help you become more aware of not only *why* you may have made certain choices in the past but also help you make better choices for decisions you might be facing now.

With this book, I hope I can help you with your healing by reminding you there is a higher power that exists within all of us. Once I began to genuinely understand the comforting nature of my spiritual home, the full landscape of eternity, I discovered that grief and joy can truly be friends.

CHAPTER 1

Bowl of Cherries

I wondered what it might be like to step into a virtual time machine and hover, slowly and deliberately, over the time line of my life. Would I hover over only the happy times, remembering the love and laughter, and then quickly bypass the unpleasant times?

Certainly, I would see some painful times along the way, but from my unique vantage point, would I be able to see exactly when and how I mustered the courage to move on? Would I wonder why some things had to happen to me at all? Would the wisdom that I had accumulated over the years allow me to see how God had slowly and deliberately guided me along and offered me a multitude of opportunities and choices? And would I understand *why* I had made those choices?

Surely, I would see times when I hadn't listened very carefully! Perhaps I had thought "my way" was the best way, so I just forged ahead. Or maybe I had listened to someone who didn't have my best interests at heart.

No doubt that all along my journey, at each of the stops, I would remember the people who had come into my life. Would I understand the reason each one had appeared and why at that particular time? Was it some divine intervention, a strange coincidence, a stroke of luck, whether good or bad? And what influence did they have on my journey?

After the death of my husband, our home was suddenly silent. I missed the comforting sounds of our daily life—dishes rattling while we fixed meals together, coffeepot perking as he prepared our morning coffee, footsteps coming down the hallway. I only heard silence, and I felt it deep within my soul. There were no voices, no footsteps, and there was only one plate at the dinner table. I was staring into a void, a void where memories and pain and loss reside, a void from which I could not imagine any escape.

As I wrestled with the bewilderment of a future that appeared to hold nothing for me, I finally decided to map out my life's time line on a blank piece of paper. I decided to take a trip on that virtual time machine, hoping to find some clues as to what might lie ahead.

I thought about growing up and how, as kids, we used to cross a cold creek by jumping from one slippery rock to the next. Eventually, we made it to the other side, but it was never without tumbling a few times and ending up wet. But then we got right back up on the next rock and continued. Once on the other side, we would jump for joy. Could it be that Tom's death was another stepping stone on my journey to the "other side?"

So my journey began.

The nearest hospital from our home was twenty miles away, and there had not been enough time to get my mother there before my birth. The one and only doctor in town, Dr. Buckingham, was summoned, and I was born at home. I arrived in this world without the bright lights, scrubbed surfaces, and antiseptic smells of a hospital, without the presence of strangers, interruptions, or the raised voices and noisy activities in hallways. I have often wondered if that at-home birth had any psychological effects on me. My mother had had no delivery complications. The familiar home environment would have been calmer, more peaceful. Over the years, my responses to experiences had seldom been ones filled with worry or anxiety. I was always trusting of others, thinking, *It's going to be okay.*

As part of the baby-boomer generation, I was born into a cold-war world of black-and-white television. The first Russian satellite was launched, the Berlin Wall was constructed, and the country was at the height of the Civil Rights Movement. Still, this isolated small town of Tidioute in Northwestern Pennsylvania sheltered us from the dysfunction in the world. But growing up in Tidioute in the 1950s and '60s ultimately played a significant role in how I dealt with death later in life.

Tidioute was bordered by a national forest and settled along the Allegheny River. Even though it was a small town, it was the home of the state's annual fishing tournament, and it attracted countless sports enthusiasts. During the summer months, tourists flocked to the hillsides for camping, hunting, and vacationing.

During those decades, my life felt very uncomplicated. There was a sense of community built upon neighbors helping neighbors, families living close together, church gatherings and school functions regularly attended by almost everyone in town, and a general feeling of security. Tidioute's population was about a thousand people, and our family was just one of many large families. I had a contented feeling of *belonging*, where acceptance and being valued were never a concern.

Our house was located on Main Street, but it was on the outskirts of town at the bottom of a long hilly road. Nearby was a small rocky creek with crystal clear water that was cold on even the hottest days of summer. The creek flowed down the valley behind our house near an oil-pumping station, under a small bridge not far from our front door, and then past my grandmother's house across the road. The distinctive sounds of the oil pumps, like heartbeats echoing through the valley, still linger as warm memories even today.

Main Street ran from the bottom of our hill for about two miles east. Although the soda fountain and penny-candy store looked like any other at that time, the quiet streets were lined with distinctive nineteenth-century Victorian houses reminiscent of the oil-boom days. During the late 1800s, Northwestern Pennsylvania was one of the greatest oil-producing states in the country.

Four generations of my family lived here, and there were almost as many relatives in town as there were fish in the river! I was in third grade, in the middle of the school year, when Dad told me we were moving to another town because he had accepted a new job. On the day we had to leave, I sat on the steps of the back porch, heartbroken, sobbing, and afraid of what was ahead. A different town one hundred miles away felt like the end of the world. Although Dad was going to work for a lumber company, we were moving to the heart of a coal mining area.

The first house we moved to was on a hillside, and there was nothing pretty about any of it. There were only three bedrooms, and the yard was too small for a family of eight. We didn't have any extended family nearby. There were no hills full of green trees, and there was no winding river dotted with canoes. All around, the ground was hard and black regardless of the season. The spirit of the town was dampened by a blanket of coal dust that appeared suspended in the air and blocked out any sunshine on most days.

I didn't like the dark school with its large grimy windows and creaky floors. The kids were all strangers, and since I was shy, it was not easy to make friends. When games were played at recess, no one asked me to join in. I felt as though I didn't belong. Grief is not always about death; it can be about a different loss. I had lost everything that was familiar to me. I had lost my home, my school, my friends, my grandmothers. It was a terribly lonely feeling, and the heaviness of it is still a vivid memory.

We lived in that house for two years, and the only good part of each year was when my brother, sister, and I went back to visit our grandmothers for two weeks during the summer. It felt good to be "home." Yahtzee was a favorite board game that we played for hours. We helped make sugar cookies that we called "yum yums." We rummaged around in their attics and spare rooms and found old pictures and toys that we treasured. The days flew by, and we were never ready to go home. The trip back was slow over winding hilly roads full of deer crossings. This provided plenty of time for me to think about all the fun we had had and wish we could have stayed longer.

Eventually, my parents found a larger house in another town. Again, the house was on a hillside, but this time, we had more land and much more room to play. Dad built a sawmill near the edge of our property, and the loud buzzing of the headsaw cutting through the logs was a daily sound. In our new yard, flowers bloomed, and the grass was green. There was plenty of room to play tag and draw large circles in the dirt for my favorite game, marbles. We cut out a baseball diamond from a field full of weeds across the road, and we played in the giant sawdust pile near the mill. The summers felt warm once again, and my sense of serenity returned.

We went to school near the center of town, which was just a mile away. It was a small mining community with rows of coal-company houses, bleak and faded, dotting the barren hillsides. There was an active coal mine across from the school. It was scary to watch the men come up out of the mineshaft. They wore helmets with small lights on the front, and their faces were black with coal. Mostly, I noticed their tired, hollow eyes. I tried to imagine how eerie it must have been so far down under the ground.

The mines produced huge smoldering piles of coal waste called *boney* piles. These piles created smelly low-hanging clouds of smoke that hung in the air like fog, and they muffled our voices as we waited for the school bus to take us home. The creek that ran near the town was the color of mustard and smelled of sulfur. The coal-mine odors were a stark contrast to the smell of freshly cut lumber at Dad's sawmill.

While I was in the sixth grade, the father of one of my classmates died accidentally at the mine. I had overheard my parents talking quietly about his dangerous job. This was the first time I had ever thought about death. I felt frightened and confused, especially when my friend cried at school. I tried to understand how she felt, but it was more than my mind could comprehend. When the teacher hugged her, we all looked at one another, but none of us knew what to say or do. It was very sad to think she would never see her dad again.

The fathers of most of our friends worked in the mines, but I was glad my dad didn't. That work seemed so much more dangerous than working at a sawmill. Our friends were always happy to come and play in our big sawdust pile instead of the smelly boney piles of coal.

There were six of us kids when we had moved. My brother Terry was a year older than me, and my sister Kathy was a year younger. Betty Ann and Dixie came next, and there was a span of ten years between Terry and our younger brother Mark. Even when we didn't have friends to play with, there was enough of us to play outdoor games like red rover, hopscotch, or ring-around-the-rosy.

It was in the middle of ninth grade when Mom and Dad told us we were moving again. Unlike the heartbroken sobs when we first moved, this time, I cried tears of joy. Dad had accepted a job managing a large lumber mill, and it was back in our hometown. Six years and two new siblings later (Julie and Alan), we were going home!

Over the years, I have traveled back to those small towns. They seemed to be haunted by the ghosts of oilmen, lumbermen, and coal miners. The oil wells were dry, and the rusty brown pumps had nearly disappeared under the brush in the overgrown fields. The black entrance holes of the coal mines were boarded shut, and the once-smoldering boney piles were hard and cold. An eerie calmness lingered over the abandoned sawmills. There was no loud buzzing of the headsaws or long, slow, hissing sounds coming from the kiln where lumber had been dried.

But whether it was the beauty of my small hometown or the loneliness of moving to new places, they each left deeply riveting impressions on me. My childhood years, beginning and ending in the same small town, were truly a smaller circle within the larger circle of my life.

*****

As I hovered over my childhood years, I warmly remembered how our home, always filled with activity, was also filled with love. I grew up accustomed to people loving me. During those formative years, I had been aware of the importance of family, and it seeped into my soul much like the thick green hillsides of my hometown silently absorbed the warm sunlight.

Mom and Dad were loving and compassionate parents. They taught us to treat everyone with kindness. I remember the time that a black truck driver from North Carolina came to the mill to pick up a load of lumber for a furniture factory. He had gone downtown to get some lunch, but he was back within a few minutes. When Dad asked him if there was a problem, he said he "couldn't get served." Dad was livid and invited him down to our house for lunch. This was my first encounter with racism. It was truly hard to understand, and it made a lasting impression on me.

Dad worked hard and was an honest man. He treated everyone with respect. I remember one time when he had heard people gossiping about how the mill really wasn't much of an economic contributor to the town. The next payday, he paid all of his employees in cash with two-dollar bills. The next stories he heard were all about how two-dollar bills were showing up all over the county!

Dad's sawmill was his sole source of income, but times were hard for a lot of families, so he sold wood and lumber to people on credit. In the end, it was all of the unpaid bills from so many families that had forced him to close the mill and move us back to my hometown.

As I grew older, I began to realize how those years had instilled a deep sense of security in me. I often referred to my childhood as "a bowl of cherries," where life was peaceful and full of fun and enjoyment. But it slowly became apparent how those years had also created an environment where I was completely unprepared for the harshness of life and the inevitable departure of those whom I had loved so much.

*****

Reflections

1. As a child, did you ever feel frightened or lonely? In what ways did those feelings affect your adult life?

   _____
   _____
   _____
   _____

2. Were you ever confronted with death as a child? Did you lose anyone you loved? If so, how did it affect you?

   _____
   _____
   _____
   _____

3. Did you feel secure as a child? Was your childhood home nurturing? How have those feelings, or the absence of them, affected you?

   _____
   _____
   _____
   _____

CHAPTER 2

Independent Thoughts

The move back to my hometown happened when I was in ninth grade. I had missed this quiet little town very much. The six years we had been gone were now, in my mind, quickly wiped away because I was so glad to be back where I was born.

One of my grandmothers lived a mile away from our new house, and my other grandmother lived only two houses away. Because the school was just across the street, we had no long bus rides to endure every day. My siblings and I were allowed to go home for lunch. That was a treat for all of us, although it must have been grueling for my mother! All twelve grades were in one building, and there were less than thirty students in my ninth-grade class.

One day after school, I walked downtown to get some groceries for my mother. While I was walking, a car went by, and some guy waved and yelled, "Hello!"

Since I was the new kid in town, I thought someone was just being friendly. I soon found out the guy was in the eleventh grade. Much to my surprise, it wasn't long before he was constantly driving around the block where we lived. He drove a blue 1959 Chevy Impala that wasn't in very good shape. It had a lot of rust spots, and the muffler had a hole in it, so it was noisy when he went by.

I was sitting on the front porch swing one evening with Dad as the Impala went past our house over and over again. Dad finally said, "Who is that idiot?"

I told him it was some guy from school, but I didn't know his name. What I didn't tell Dad was that I loved the attention!

A few days later, we met in a hallway at school, and he introduced himself. His name was Tom, and he lived across the river. His family had moved here from Pittsburgh a few years before because they had grown tired of the city. His father had built one of the nicest restaurants in the area. I had never been there because my family always had dinners at home. Mom and Dad said it had a good reputation for serving delicious home-cooked meals.

I was instantly swept away by Tom's story and his kind eyes and gentle manner. We soon started dating regularly—or as regularly as I was permitted. Since I was the eldest girl in the family, dating was new territory, and lots of disagreements ensued between my parents and me about reasonable rules and boundaries. Why did my brother, who was only one year older than me, not get the same scrutiny I did? I would rarely meet my unrealistic curfews and would subsequently end up being forbidden to go out the following weekend. There were absolutely no dates on weeknights.

I could tell Mom liked Tom. She always smiled when she greeted him. He was a little embarrassed but at ease as she kidded him about driving around our block so often. She made it a point to make him feel comfortable when he came to the house. Dad was the more suspicious one.

After Dad got established at his new job running the sawmill, he needed to hire help for work in the lumberyard. Tom was big and strong and eager, so Dad hired him. I sometimes wondered if he wasn't hired just so Dad could keep an eye on him. But Tom was a good employee, and they began to get along. Our negotiations over dating rules got a little smoother, and I simply didn't have a care in the world. Tom, on the other hand, was more of a rebel and always at odds with his father. His dad wanted him to spend more time at the restaurant, but he preferred working with lumber instead of waiting on tables, and they frequently argued about it.

When Tom became a senior, we started seriously talking about getting married. He reminded me about that first day he had seen me walking downtown when he had driven by and yelled out the window. He said he knew then we would get married one day!

With eight kids in our family, I knew there was probably no money for college, but I had started researching one in Buffalo, New York, and another one in Pittsburgh. I had two aunts who were very independent women, and each time I visited them, I had an ever-increasing desire to leave town after graduation and see some of the world. Certainly, I wanted to get married eventually, but for the time being, I kept those *worldly* thoughts to myself.

Aunt Mamie, my great-aunt, had originally taught school back in the days when only single women could be teachers. Now she was nearing retirement after working thirty years for JCPenney. She started at the company in the mid-1930s and had risen to the level of supervisor. I never knew her husband, who had died many years earlier. She lived alone, but even after retirement, she dressed up every day as if she were still going to work. She always wore a pretty dress with matching necklace, earrings, lipstick, and high-heeled shoes. She exuded confidence, and she loved talking about the increasing opportunities for women.

My aunt Marty lived across the street from us. She and her husband had both served in the US Air Force for several years. They lived in Virginia with their three young children. One tragic day, her husband and two-year-old son perished in a drowning accident on the Potomac River in Washington, DC. After that horrible accident, she moved back to our town, where she was closer to her mother and siblings.

Often, when I visited her, she would talk about losing her husband and her little boy, how the canoe had upset for some unknown reason. It made me uncomfortable because I didn't know what to say, and my heart ached. I could not imagine coping with such a loss. Her life had been permanently changed in an instant, and she was faced with making a new life for herself and her two other children.

I thought of the sadness at the death of my school friend's dad at the coal mine a few years before, but this was the death of a child. Why would God allow a little boy to drown? How was a mother supposed to deal with such pain while raising two other small children?

Why couldn't little Stevie have had the chance to grow up? How do you explain to the other children that they aren't going to ever see their daddy or their little brother again? All of this felt intensely unfair. It left me with more questions than answers.

Feeling sad and confused, I watched my aunt pick up the pieces of her life. She moved into a house across the street from ours, and she enrolled her kids in school. She usually had lots of visitors because we had so much family in town. As she tackled a life of raising a family by herself, I often wondered where she found the strength.

Both of these aunts loved Tom. He always made a point of visiting them whenever he could, and they enjoyed his company. He loved to talk and laugh and kid around, and they both got a kick out of him.

After he graduated, Tom enlisted in the navy. Although it was during the Vietnam War, I was hopeful that being in this branch of the service would keep him away from any danger. I thought perhaps he would be assigned to a ship instead of going into combat. While this was a time when many young men were trying to avoid the draft, Tom freely enlisted. His older brother had been in the navy, and Tom wanted to follow in his footsteps. Little did he know how this choice would impact the remainder of his life.

As he waited to report for duty, Tom continued to work at the mill. One afternoon, someone from the fire department came looking for him to tell him his dad had just died of a heart attack at the restaurant. It was a devastating shock to everyone, but Tom was overwhelmed with guilt. He and his dad had had another argument the night before, and they had never resolved it.

Tom became a different person after the death of his father. He was much quieter and more serious, the turmoil of his guilt and regrets compounding his grief. I struggled with these changes in him as I tried to imagine life without my dad.

I really missed Tom's belly laugh. It seemed as though he had always been laughing. We actually got thrown out of a theater one time because he was laughing so loudly that no one could hear the movie! With four generations of my large family living within five miles, I used to tease him by saying that I dated him because he was the only guy in town not related to me. Oh, how he laughed! But his laughter was gone now, replaced by a heavy silence filled with sadness.

We were raised in the Presbyterian church, which was just down the street from our house. I remember listening to sermons where heaven and hell were presented as the only two *options* after people died. After the death of Tom's father, I contemplated these options more seriously. Heaven was definitely where I wanted to go, but it still felt so final. I had a lot of questions about dying, but I was too afraid to hear the answers…so I didn't ask. But I wondered, if death was *forever*, what exactly did *forever* mean? What happens after someone dies? Are they sad because they are away from the people they had loved? Can they still see me?

Religion was an important part of growing up. Sunday-school classes, attending church, and singing in the choir all had positive effects on me as a child and young adult.

Learning the Golden Rule at an early age was incredibly important. "Treating others the way I wanted to be treated" didn't feel complicated. Acquiring a set of values such as compassion, honesty, and hard work were not only taught to me through my religion; my parents were shining examples of it. Learning to pray was not only a peaceful experience; it gave me confidence that things would be okay.

When it was time for Tom to leave for his formal enlistment in Pittsburgh, I went with him and stayed overnight with his sister, who still lived there. The next morning, we said a very tearful goodbye, and I went back home alone—alone. I shuddered. Although Tom was not going away forever like his father, it was startling to realize that when I got home, he would not be there. It was unsettling to think how different my life was going to be without him.

During my remaining two years of high school, I really didn't date much; maybe an occasional ride or movie with someone, but everyone knew I was Tom's girl. I wrote to him almost every day, and he wrote when he could. He had been assigned to a mobile construction battalion known as the Seabees. This was not the assignment on a ship that I had hoped for, but he loved construction work, so this pleased him.

Tom's letters made me smile when he wrote about the fun times we had had during the summers. Simple things like going for rides, visiting our favorite ice cream stand, and going on picnics and to drive-in movies had kept us happy.

The community soda foundation was called The Chocolate Shop, and it was our favorite hangout. It had a long, narrow room that housed a few groceries like milk and bread in the front of the building near the cash register. As you walked farther back, six high red vinyl-covered stools lined the counter, and behind it was a long greasy grill and a fountain drink machine.

In the back of the room were about a dozen tables and a juke-box that blared loudly on the weekends until closing time. I thought about all the good times Tom and I had had sitting at those tables, his infectious belly laugh entertaining everyone. We met friends there and talked for hours, sipping on "fresh lime," a sugary drink made with simple syrup, club soda, and a freshly squeezed lime. It replaced Coca-Cola for quite a while, and we all felt older as we thought we were drinking a more alcoholic beverage!

We sang along to our favorite songs playing on the jukebox. Tom's choice was usually "Unchained Melody" by the Righteous Brothers. It was "our song," and in the years ahead, regardless of the circumstances, it became a reminder of the love we had shared.

Every summer, the town's population swelled as hundreds of *flatlanders* arrived for their annual vacations. Flatlanders were the tourists who came from faraway cities and neighboring states where we thought the scenery could not begin to rival the magnificent hills that surrounded our town. I remember floating down the river in a canoe one afternoon with one of my younger brothers. I will never forget him saying that the hills were so green, they made his eyes feel good.

As the flatlanders settled in, the hillsides were brimming with tents and campsites, and the winter-worn cottages bounced back to life with those seeking refuge from their normal routines. Those days, the river was dotted with canoes and rowboats, some homemade and looking as though they could sink at any minute. People of all ages splashed their hands and feet in the cool water and lazily floated on old inner tubes. And long into the warm humid nights, campfires flickered across the countryside like a yard full of lightning bugs.

Before Tom worked at his dad's restaurant or my dad's sawmill, he worked part-time at the local grocery store. Summers were the height of the season for the store. In his letters, he wrote about how the cash register bells rang constantly, and cash drawers popped open loudly. Stiff brown paper bags crackled as he packed them with hot dogs, marshmallows, and cold soda pop. I could feel his memories of our happy days together.

As teenagers, Tom and I both loved and hated this foreign influx of strangers. The Chocolate Shop buzzed with new energy as the nightly boisterous crowds spilled out onto the sidewalk. Business was once again brisk at the local hardware, which was now well stocked with charcoal and fishing supplies. Oftentimes, folks had trouble finding a parking spot along the downtown street as streams of traffic came in from across the bridge and down the hilly winding roads that led into town.

This brought a new excitement to our small town, but it also meant that some of the town's teenage couples broke up as these out-of-town kids were here for some summer romance! After the flatlanders left and school started in the fall, the town shrunk back to its normal size, and the excitement waned. During the day, the Chocolate Shop turned into a place that was mostly frequented by the old folks who would stop by to have a cup of coffee and read the newspaper or just gossip.

There were not many other things to do in town. Directly across the street from the Chocolate Shop was a small dilapidated movie theater. It was only open on weekends, cost fifty cents to get in, and held about fifty people. If a movie like *Psycho* was playing, I was not interested in going! Tom loved Western movies, so we watched ones like *How the West Was Won* or *Spencer's Mountain*. The aroma of freshly popped popcorn mixed with the smell of hamburgers and fries sizzling at the Chocolate Shop.

In one of Tom's letters, he reminded me of how we used to laugh about the time I snuck out of the house and met him at the movies. Once Mom and Dad realized I was gone, they came looking for me and found us at the theater, where I was promptly taken home and grounded for another week!

There was a bowling alley across the river located not far from the restaurant Tom's father had built. His family sold the restaurant after his dad's death, and seeing the dark and empty building was a harsh reminder of the loneliness left behind.

This beautiful small country town that I loved so much was actually beginning to feel too small. Life was changing. Tom's letters reinforced my yearning to be a part of a larger world. I was feeling a restlessness that dampened the contentment that had been such a big part of my life.

I truly missed Tom, and I found it very difficult to fill the summer nights that we had loved so much. My friend Harriet, my sister Kathy, and I were all bored with *everything* one night, and we just needed a different place to go to for fun. But where would that be? None of us had a car. A lot of brainstorming led to the idea of creating a new hangout. What about church? Our big church, located on Main Street, was bordered by an empty alley on one side and the preacher's manse (not too close) on the other side. Behind the church was a small hill that led down to the railroad tracks, and then the river was just beyond. The Sunday-school room was in the basement at the back of the church with its own entrance. It was a perfect location for the privacy that teenagers crave. So we talked our pastor into letting us clear out the Sunday-school room every Saturday afternoon and, of course, put it all back together late that night.

Kathy and I located some old ice chests in our garage, and then the three of us talked our parents into lending us enough money to buy some ice and a few cases of soda pop and potato chips. But most importantly, we approached a classmate, Billy, who had an extensive collection of 45-rpm records: "California Dreamin'," "Dancing in the Street," "I Heard It through the Grapevine"—you name it, Billy had it! No one else in the entire county could match his assortment of popular music.

Billy was a quiet and reserved guy; actually, *strange* was the more common opinion. He never joined in on any conversations, so he didn't have many friends. It was well known that his record collection was sacred to him. When we approached him with our idea, our excitement was contagious enough to persuade him to help us out. Of course, he would be the only person to actually play his records at the new hangout.

We decided to call our new business "The Spot," and our advertising was all by word of mouth. We cleared the floor for dancing and set up as many folding chairs as we could find around the outside edges of the room. For dimmer lighting, we brought in two small tables and lamps from home. Billy's record player was set up in one corner with long wires leading to a speaker on each side of the room. We filled two large ice chests with soda pop, set up a table for potato chips, and placed a cigar box on a small table at the back door for the twenty-five-cent admission fee to cover our costs.

The place was overflowing on opening night! The music blared, and we ran out of soda pop and chips in no time at all. We stayed open for several weeks and even had kids from neighboring towns come and hang out once in a while. When the weather got too cold, we closed, paid our parents back, and split a small profit among the three of us. We each gave Billy part of our share.

This first entrepreneurial experience was enough to stir an already adventurous spirit in me. We had enthusiastically taken an idea and built upon it to make something happen out of practically nothing. If we could turn a quiet little town into a cool place to be every Saturday night, think of the possibilities beyond its boundaries!

My thoughts turned to graduation, and my dreams of adventure took an exciting turn. During my senior year, Tom received orders for Vietnam. His construction unit had been attached to a marine division to build housing for the troops as they moved through the jungles. I was scared to death, and although Tom didn't admit it, I knew he was also frightened. He was a nineteen-year-old kid from a small country town. What did he know about living and potentially fighting in a jungle?

Fortunately, he was able to come home on leave before he shipped out to Vietnam. As we sat on the front porch swing one evening, he pulled an engagement ring out of his pocket and asked me to marry him. Of course, I said yes! Thoughts of college—or whatever I thought I was going to do after graduation— completely left my mind. All I knew at that moment was that I loved him. Suddenly, the ominous cloud of war hanging over our heads disappeared while we planned our life together.

Once Tom was in Vietnam, his letters were sporadic. That winter on Christmas Eve, he somehow managed to call me using an amateur radio (also known as a ham radio). I couldn't believe it! He sounded so far away, and the line was full of static. Every time one of us said something, we had to say, "Over," for our message to be transmitted. It was a strange and awkward way to talk, but I was thrilled to hear his voice if only for a few minutes.

The rest of my senior year was uneventful, and I couldn't wait to graduate. With every day that went by, I grew more restless. I knew there was no future for me in this town, and Tom still had two years to serve in the navy.

It was the summer of 1966, and the protests against the Vietnam War were rapidly increasing. Already this year, there had been more military casualties than the year before, and it looked as if there was no end to the conflict in sight. Although Tom was not directly involved in any combat, he was exposed to the hot, rainy jungle and the *unknown* as he patrolled the camp perimeters at night.

It was disturbing to watch the news reports of people protesting while their fellow citizens were dying in a dangerous far-off jungle. Even though some protestors were actually protesting *against* the government for going to war and *for* the veterans who were fighting and dying, it oftentimes was not perceived that way by those stationed there. Tom wrote about how angry he became when he heard of the protests. He and many of his buddies felt as though their country was not supporting them. The war was tearing the country apart. It felt like everyone was on one side or the other, with very few in the middle. It was a violent, chaotic, and confusing time. It felt as though a demarcation line had been drawn in our history.

INDEPENDENT THOUGHTS

The crossroad I was facing required an important decision. The two choices I had were simply to stay or to go. I knew Tom wanted me to stay at home and wait for him to return, but he wasn't here for us to talk about it.

I thought about the career Aunt Mamie had, one that had been slowly paving the way for other women to follow. I thought about Aunt Marty. Even though her life had changed drastically after the death of her husband and son, she had traveled across the country and visited places I had only read about.

My thoughts also turned to the excitement I had felt when we had created "The Spot." With an idea and some creative work, we had brought happiness to all who had come to hang out on weekends. What other incredible opportunities might there be beyond this small town? What do I want to experience? How do I want to express myself?

In the end, I found the courage to do what my soul had been whispering to me.

*****

I hovered over this second stop on my virtual tour for quite a while. As children, we are frequently affected by the choices that are made by others. The move away from my hometown when I was in third grade was an early manifestation of loss. The idyllic surroundings of that early childhood home were in stark contrast to what I had experienced in a new home in a different town. There, I was faced with a new reality, and even if subconsciously, I chose to not like it.

Once we moved back to my hometown, my happiest days became the ones with Tom. But those days eventually turned into a more solemn, sobering view of life. The death of his father changed him from a jovial, playful young man into a more restrained person who was then catapulted into a war in the middle of a jungle.

The shock and grief that he felt when his father had died were intensified by his feelings of guilt. The unresolved argument they had had the night before haunted him. The regret that he felt for not settling their dispute was deeply painful. Much like the death of Aunt Marty's husband and son, there had been no goodbyes.

I was in the eleventh grade when Tom left for the navy. His absence was starting to change me. I had spent all of my days with him, happy and carefree. But now I started wondering who I really was and what I wanted to experience.

I had loved talking to both Aunt Mamie and Aunt Marty about their careers. These two strong-willed women constantly encouraged me to get away from home after graduation and to experience things that our small town could never offer.

Tom was my first love, and it was perfect. It was innocent and powerful. It created an important foundation for years to come, but I had no idea just how naive I was. The innocence of that love, the simplicity of the small-town environment, and the excitement of what might exist beyond it overshadowed the faraway war.

Looking back, I could see how I had grown to know a God who was loving, a God who knows everything we are capable of doing, a God who knows who belongs in our life, a God who creates a path for each of us to follow and gives us the free will to choose how we will respond.

Believing there was a "higher power" that could be trusted was comforting. Although I was taught to *follow* God, it would be many years later that I actually realized that God had been following me. He knew where I was and what was happening at all times, and he put opportunities out in front of me, giving me choices that would define who I would become.

Yes, I could see where God definitely had a hand in all of it. As my life unfolded and choices were made, there would be some extraordinary turns of events.

*****

Reflections

1. What role do you think your first love played in your future relationships?

   _____
   _____
   _____
   _____

2. Did you experience the death of anyone close to you as a young adult? If so, how did it affect you?

   _____
   _____
   _____
   _____

3. Our childhood homes help shape us into who we are and what we think is important. Describe how your home life is still a part of you.

   _____
   _____
   _____
   _____

CHAPTER 3

Leaving Home

Shortly before high school graduation, I decided that I would never be happy if I didn't somehow get out on my own. Staying at or near home would mean I needed to get some sort of clerical or sales job. Although more opportunities were becoming available to women, teaching and nursing were still the most prominent careers available. Even if I had had an interest in either one of those professions, both required a higher education, and that was out of the question because of the cost of tuition.

Although Tom would be out of the navy in two years, it felt like a long time to wait while working at a place where my growth would feel limited. Yes, I loved him, and we would remain engaged, but I had to leave that small town. I decided to join the US Air Force. My enlistment would be for four years, and since Tom would be gone for half of that time, I rationalized that it would take him a couple of years to get financially set for us to get married.

My parents were not excited about my decision, especially Mom. I was the eldest daughter and the first to leave home. My older brother had been drafted into the army but had not left home yet. I knew she was worried about Tom, and now she would worry about two of her own children.

The little I knew about the air force I had heard from Aunt Marty. I don't remember what her job was while she was enlisted, but she had been stationed in California, and that was enough for me! It was out of Tidioute and part of that larger world I had been thinking about. Two weeks after graduation, I was on my way to Pittsburgh to enlist. Needless to say, Tom was not happy when I wrote and told him, but this was something I was determined to do, and I was sure he would understand eventually.

Mom and Dad drove me to Pittsburgh to catch a plane to San Antonio, Texas, and I checked into the hotel room that had been reserved for me. It was another tearful goodbye, but my excitement kept me up all night because I had never flown on an airplane. I was sworn in the next morning at the recruiting office, along with about a dozen others. Sarah was the only other girl in our group.

A uniformed sergeant drove us to the airport to board a Pan American airplane. It was known as the "World's Most Experienced Airline," and I was too excited to be intimated by the size of the airport or the long lines of people and piles of luggage waiting at the gates. Everyone was dressed up as though they were going to church. Men wore suits, and the women all wore dresses.

Sarah and I sat together and held hands as the plane took off. We were fascinated with the airline stewardesses. They were dressed in identical blue skirt suits with pillbox hats, and they wore white gloves and high heels. They were so polite and interested in where we were going. I felt extremely important!

Sarah and I talked all the way to Chicago, which is where we had to change planes. I often wondered what happened to her because she missed the next flight, and I never saw her again.

Basic training at Lackland Air Force Base lasted six weeks, and the days went by quickly. There were daily white-glove inspections at 4:45 a.m., where we stood at attention by our bedsides, waiting for the dormitory chief to come by. She would inspect all furniture, baseboards, and floors by wiping her white-gloved hand across them. If she found any dust, the room needed to be cleaned again and reinspected.

The mornings were filled with classroom studies on a barrage of military rules and regulations. In the afternoons, we marched out on the drill pad for what felt like hours. Evenings consisted of endless dormitory duties. Our cotton fatigue uniforms had to be hand-washed using liquid starch so that once they were ironed, they stood up by themselves. This was certainly a catch-22 for all of us because after sitting in a classroom all morning, the stiff-starched skirt put a snag or hole in our nylon stockings. And when that happened, we were written up for being out of uniform!

While standing at attention one day to collect my weekly pay, the sergeant in charge noticed that a button on my uniform was not fastened. As a result of such a minor oversight, I was ordered to write a five-hundred-word essay on why buttons are put on girls' blouses! This all seemed quite silly after hearing Tom talk about his grueling boot camp, where he had to learn how to handle various weapons and endure intense physical training.

A black flag was raised any day that was too hot to be outside, so on those days, we had more classroom studies. Mail call was the best part of the day because I always heard from someone at home. Hardly a day went by when I didn't hear from my parents or younger siblings or my grandmothers or various aunts. They always wrote about how much they missed me and asked what I was doing. I had to laugh each time they said there was nothing new at home! Years later, I thought how getting all that mail must have kept me from getting homesick.

It was sad to see some of the girls become disappointed when they didn't receive any mail, and that happened a lot. My sudden exposure to so many strangers taught me that not everyone had the peaceful childhood I had enjoyed. There were stories of abuse, fights, loneliness, and fear, and I had difficulty comprehending them. Alcohol played a large part in many of their stories. I had not really thought about it before because there was never any alcohol at our home as I was growing up. I felt extremely grateful for that and for knowing I had so many people who loved me.

During my basic training period, there were two people who died by suicide. I never knew how they had died, but I wondered how anything could be so terrible that a person would actually choose to die. Death was so final; surely that could not be the best option. I struggled to reconcile all of the pain and sadness around me.

LEAVING HOME

After basic training, I was assigned to Amarillo AFB, which was located in the Texas Panhandle. This location was famous for its unpredictable weather patterns, with massive temperature changes on a daily basis, raging winds, and long periods of drought. I was assigned to attend school for an administrative-specialist position. It looked like I might end up being a secretary after all, and I was disappointed about that prospect. It was a three-month course where students were allowed to work at their own pace. I finished in nine days.

With excellent grades, I was eligible to choose a general geographic area for a permanent assignment. I chose to be on the east coast, and I hoped that I might get assigned to the New England area. This would be fairly close to home and probably helpful as Tom and I planned our future together.

While I waited for my orders, I had plenty of free time. It was October, and although the winds were strong and cold, I walked around the base for hours each day. There was nothing appealing about the base. The landscape was flat and barren and the drab military buildings all looked the same. So much had happened since I left home; sometimes it felt like I was wandering in a strange world, all the while wondering what would happen next.

Amarillo AFB was part of the Strategic Air Command, and it was home to the giant B-52 bomber aircraft. Because they flew over the jungles of Vietnam, they were painted camouflaged military green, brown, and black. These planes took off and landed constantly, day and night. I was mesmerized by their sheer size and ominous mission. Every time I watched one, I worried about Tom. He must have seen these same bombers fly overhead but with a much more sinister mission. For the very first time, as I watched these planes come and go, the war suddenly felt more real, more present, and much more frightening. I wondered what Tom was doing.

After several days, my orders arrived, and I was assigned to Eglin AFB, Florida. Although I had hoped for a base closer to home, I was headed for a part of the country I had never seen. That familiar stir of excitement was back!

Before traveling to Florida, I went home for a month to visit my family. Being there felt as though I had traveled back through a time tunnel. I was surrounded by the love of my family instead of the sad stories I had heard for the past few months. And the peacefulness of the countryside was a stark contrast to the B-52 bombers I had watched screaming down the flight lines. I was reminded of the glaring contrasts that came with each new reality.

When I arrived in Florida, once again I noticed the striking change in the landscape. The dusty Texas prairie was replaced with swaying palm trees, and the warm sunshine quickly wiped out my memory of the cold winter wind. I knew instantly I would like it here.

After I finished my first week of work, I wanted to visit the beaches that everyone talked about. I didn't own a car, so my best choice was the base bus. After boarding the bus, I found the seats were hard and torn, with yellow stuffing coming out. Only a few of the windows would open. It was hot and noisy, but it was free, and I was grateful to have the transportation.

About fifteen minutes down the road, the driver passed a paved parking lot filled with expensive new cars. There was an impressive-looking building with red carpet that covered the front steps and a walkway to a valet station. The windows had long drapes, and I was sure the building was air-conditioned. I was thrilled at the sight of it, but the sign out front read, "Officers' Club." Since officers had a college degree, and I had enlisted just out of high school, I was somewhat disheartened as the bus continued farther down the road.

Soon, the driver turned into another parking lot and stopped in front of a smaller building. This parking lot had weeds sticking up through the cracks in the asphalt and mostly older model cars in it. The building was more exposed to the heat with large screened windows. I noticed a sign out front that read, "Non-Commissioned Officers' Club." I knew a non-commissioned officer didn't necessarily have a college education but had been in the service long enough to obtain a fairly high rank. Since I had only served a few months, I stayed on the bus as it continued down the road.

LEAVING HOME

It eventually made another turn and headed down a narrow road that was full of potholes. I was the only person left on the bus, and the driver, looking somewhat annoyed, yelled back to me, "This is where you get off!"

I stepped off the bus and turned toward the beach. I saw a post stuck in the sand with a small sign nailed on it. The words were nearly illegible because of wind and sand erosion. As I got closer, I saw "Enlisted Airmen's Club" roughly carved out on it. I looked around, and I didn't see a parking lot, a red carpet, a patio, not even a Coke machine. Instead, I saw an outdoor portable outhouse tipped to one side. I thought, *This just isn't right!*

The bus returned late that afternoon, and hot, thirsty, and sunburned, I rode back to the base. This first visit to the beach was unexpectedly a lesson in the social classes within the military. I thought about the paved parking lot at the Officers' Club, the weeds growing in the parking lot at the Non-Commissioned Officers' Club, and then the narrow bumpy road to the Enlisted Airmen's Club. I realized that I was on the bottom step of a career ladder, and I was now intensely determined to start my long climb.

I was assigned to the data-processing department as a keypunch operator; the IBM keypunch and verifier machines were my introduction to modern technology. These machines punched information into stiff paper cards. Each card had eighty columns and twelve rows with each individual punched column representing a letter of the alphabet, a special character, or a number. This was one of the earliest forms of storing information that was subsequently read by larger accounting machines and computers. I worked the day shift, and within a few months, I worked my way up to lead operator. Personnel from different agencies on the base constantly brought boxes of miscellaneous paper forms, such as warehouse inventories, payroll time sheets, jet fuel usage logs, etc. to my office. I had to create a unique program card that contained the format of each of the different forms. The card was then wrapped around a small drum at the top center of the machine before the individual forms could be keyed. This daily routine of creating program cards and keying the punched cards with information from the various forms became rather boring, but it sparked my curiosity. I wanted to understand *what happened* to those cards after they left our shop.

Lois was the sergeant who came to pick up the punched cards each day, and I quickly got acquainted with her. I asked a lot of questions, and she eventually invited me back to her office. It was located in the same building, but it was in a larger room full of strange-looking machines. These machines were of varying sizes, but they were all noisy, and punched cards were moving in and out of them. I was awestruck! Suddenly, I had a riveting glimpse of an exciting future, and I realized what my aunts had been talking about. There were, indeed, new and thrilling opportunities for women. *This* was why I had to leave my family, my small town…and, sadly, Tom.

Lois became both my mentor and my good friend. Once she saw that my interest and motivation were genuine, she also became a taskmaster. She challenged me with assignments that were far too difficult for anyone who was just learning about automation.

Shortly, my eight-hour days turned into sixteen-hour days. I worked at my keypunching job during the day and then another eight hours in the "machine room." Under Lois's direction, I worked in the magnetic tape library where I learned how to log, schedule, and retrieve tapes for computer jobs that were scheduled to run the next day. There were hundreds of tapes. The thousands of punched cards that we keyed each day were the original source of information that was read by the computer and subsequently stored on these tapes. Most computer jobs then read information on these input tapes and wrote updated information back out on an output tape. Each large spool of tape had 2,400 feet of one-inch tape. I was genuinely astounded by what I was learning.

Next, I learned how to operate the punched card accounting machines. These machines performed various functions by reading the punched cards that came out of my keypunch unit and producing stand-alone reports that did not require updated information from the main computer. One of the machines simply sorted the cards in different sequences. Another machine read the cards and printed accounting reports. But before the reports could be produced, the control panel in the back of the machine had to be hard-wired to add, subtract, multiply, divide, or perform other mathematical computations. There was a collator machine that read cards from two feeders and combined them based on certain wired functions. Even though I absorbed an enormous amount of information, I still couldn't seem to get enough. The sights, the sounds, and the automated functions were intoxicating!

Eventually, I worked in the production control office, where the reports produced by the computer were checked for accuracy, separated, and sent to the agencies that had brought the paper forms to be keypunched. Another large machine called a *decollator* was used to separate multipart reports by stripping out the carbon backing. A total of six copies could be separated at one time. It was certainly noisy and messy, but it was the final step performed before getting new and updated information back to the agencies.

Each time I asked Lois a question, she asked, "Well, what do you think?" Then I would have to figure it out on my own or admit that I couldn't do it (which was not an option). She knew my ultimate goal was to see what went on in the computer room located down the hall. I was more than intrigued by the sign on the door that read, "Authorized Access Only."

Six months after I arrived in Florida, Tom was home on leave from Vietnam for two weeks. We made plans for him to come and visit me for a few days. The anticipation of seeing him turned to profound sadness after he arrived. Who was this guy? After Tom's dad died, he had become much more reserved; he had lost his famous belly laugh. But this time was different. There was a faraway look in his eyes. It felt as though I was with a complete stranger. We struggled to have a meaningful conversation.

After a few days, we both agreed that staying engaged was not a good idea. After all, who knew what the future held? Before he left, we agreed to remain friends. I thought for many years that he was simply angry because I had joined the air force. As time would teach me, I was dreadfully wrong.

After a few weeks, I began dating again, but I didn't really enjoy it. There were certainly plenty of guys on the base, but I never met anyone who was as much fun as Tom used to be. Mostly, I worked overtime, and I buried myself in a career that I was determined would validate my decision to leave home.

As I was wiring one of the accounting machines one evening, the supervisor of the computer room came out and invited me to come back and look around. My heart stopped! As I walked past the "Authorized Access Only" sign on the computer room door, I felt my world changing again. I stood in awe of the IBM 1401 mainframe computer. It filled the room. Magnetic tape drives were spinning back and forth as the information was read and written. The disk drum unit was humming as information was accessed by mechanical arms moving in and out between the stack of disks. Because of all the heat generated by the equipment, the air-conditioned room was always cold, but it was magical!

I spent many evenings in the computer room. I had learned what happened to the punched cards once they left my office. I had learned the mechanics of how the accounting machines worked and how the computer could read and write magnetic tapes and access information on disk drums. I now wondered, *"What* exactly is making this computer do the work? How does it know what and when to read and write?"

The faith that Lois had in me was inspiring. Since she was highly respected by all the team members, I was certainly grateful but somewhat surprised that she gave me so much attention. Certainly, my excitement and motivation were genuine, and I felt them deep in my soul. But Lois's positive attitude was such an inspiration for me to always make the best of any opportunity.

She was single and a few years older than me, and she outranked me by several stripes. She lived in a town a few miles off base with her mother, who was an alcoholic, and her younger sister, who was mentally challenged. Her father had left them many years before, so she was the sole provider for her family. Although we seldom did anything socially, I visited her and her family on most weekends. Once I saw what she was faced with at home, I had even more admiration for her.

Sometimes it was difficult to believe that I was learning so much, and Tom was in a war halfway around the world. I began to wonder about God's plans for us. Life had felt so simple just a couple of years ago, but the choices we had both made had dramatically altered our lives. The simplicity of growing up was now a distant memory. I was sure Tom felt the same way because when he came to visit me, we talked about those years, and his eyes had filled with tears.

While I was stationed in Florida, a close friend of mine from back home died unexpectedly. Judy was only twenty years old when she died from food poisoning after eating Easter dinner. I was shocked and felt numb when I got the phone call.

Judy was the cousin of a school friend, and we had met when she was visiting one summer. She drove a Ford Mustang that we used to ride around in on the weekends. Because she lived in a bigger town about sixty miles away, she had more things to talk about. I used to tell her how I hoped to get away on my own one day, and she had always encouraged me to leave town after graduation.

On the flight home to attend her funeral, I thought about my grade-school friend who had lost her father in the mining accident. That death had saddened me. I thought about how Tom's father had died so suddenly from a heart attack. That death had frightened me. I thought about how Aunt Marty had lost her husband and little boy. Those deaths seemed so unfair. I thought about the suicides on base when I was stationed in Florida. Those deaths felt so preventable. Now with Judy's death, more than anything, I was angry. My reactions to death differed according to the circumstances, but they didn't wipe away my fear of the ultimate finality of it.

Each time I received a letter from Judy, she had always said how proud she was of me for joining the air force. Because of that, I wore my uniform to her funeral. I remember very little about the service or the gathering of friends and family at her mother's home afterward. What I do remember is leaving the cemetery, sitting in the back seat of the car, looking back at the grave site. Suddenly, I saw an unearthly transparent image of Judy standing next to her grave. She was looking at me and saluting. I was so dazed by the vision that I closed my eyes and looked again. She was gone. When I told my family what I had seen, they didn't believe me. I'm sure some of them thought

I was just overcome with grief, which, in the moment, I thought was quite possible. However, I would eventually learn, through other experiences, just how real this heavenly sign actually was.

After I returned to the base, I was notified to report to the central personnel department. I was somewhat nervous as I walked into the office because I had no idea what to expect. As it turned out, with only one year left in the air force, I was offered reassignment to Hickam AFB in Hawaii. The only caveat was that it was a three-year tour of duty, and that meant I would have to extend my current enlistment for an additional two years.

As I read and reread the requirements for the assignment, I wondered if I would ever get another chance to go to Hawaii. It sounded so exotic. I had heard about people who saved money all of their lives to travel there. But more importantly, wouldn't this give me more time to prepare for a career in technology?

I thought about my two aunts who had influenced my decision to join the air force. They had both been confronted with difficult choices in their lives, and they had taken advantage of available opportunities. Here I was faced with an opportunity they could have only dreamed about.

I signed the extension papers, and I awaited my orders.

*****

At this third hovering stop on my virtual tour, my thoughts returned to the war and how it had changed Tom. Although he and I had separated as friends, we no longer stayed in touch with each other. After he came to visit me in Florida, I had heard he volunteered for another year in Vietnam.

Having completed his enlistment in the navy, he was now home and working. I was not surprised to hear he was working in the construction business, but I was surprised and saddened to hear he had a serious drinking problem.

My sister Kathy's husband had also recently returned home after serving in Vietnam. He had been in the army infantry and was heavily involved in combat. He, too, had been struggling with alcohol addiction, but he was also suffering from nightmares and flashbacks of the war. He was angry at the protests shown on television. Kathy told me how badly he had been treated when he got home. Returning veterans were spat upon and called murderers and "baby killers." Had this happened to Tom too?

The war had far-reaching tentacles. Entire families struggled with the mental, emotional, and physical damage inflicted upon the men and women who had served. As they returned to civilian life, the war raged on in their minds. Like Tom, some of them had volunteered to join the military, but most of them had been drafted and left with no choice.

I wondered what life might have been like if I had finished my last year of duty in Florida and then gone back home. I even started wondering if my own excitement about leaving home—and Tom—had really been a selfish choice. It was painful to think I might have contributed to his struggles.

But if I had gone home and we had been married, how would I have handled his unexpected behavior? Would our marriage have survived? Although there were these moments of guilt, and I had more questions than answers, I did not regret the choice I had made.

Lois had given me opportunities I could never have imagined. I was actually grateful that I could not afford the tuition to go to college after high school; otherwise, I would not have joined the air force, met Lois, and been introduced to the world of technology. I realized she was one of many people whom God had gently placed on my path.

And the sudden death of Judy had stirred an old familiar fear.

*****

Reflections

1. What were your dreams when you were young? What did you hope to do with your life?

   _____
   _____
   _____
   _____

2. Think of a choice you have made that was based upon *no* previous experience? Could you have made a better choice? Think of a choice you have made that *was* based upon previous experience. Did you have a better outcome?

   _____
   _____
   _____
   _____

3. Think of an important choice that you have made. Was that choice made using information from your mind, or did you listen to the smaller voice of your soul?

   _____
   _____
   _____
   _____

CHAPTER 4

Trouble in Paradise

Tora! Tora! Tora! was an epic film about the 1941 bombing of Pearl Harbor, released in 1970. But in January 1969, as I stepped onto the tarmac at Honolulu International Airport from my San Francisco flight, I saw several of the infamous Japanese Rising Sun torpedo bombers flying very low overhead. I stopped dead in my tracks and even stooped down a little until I heard laughter and someone calling my name. I turned around and saw two women who were obviously my *sponsors*. They were not in uniform, but I was expecting someone to welcome me and to make sure I had no problems at my new living quarters. Being greeted by the filming of that movie was quite a welcome indeed, and it gave those two women something to tease me about for the next three years!

After having three roommates in Florida, I was now thrilled to have a room to myself. My orders directed me to report to the Pacific Air Command Headquarters at 8:00 a.m. on Monday, so that meant I had the weekend to settle in. On Sunday afternoon, I set out to locate the office because I didn't want to be late for work the next day. Along the way, I noticed numerous holes in the concrete buildings, which I later learned were the bullet holes from the attack on Pearl Harbor. It was unnerving when I had gotten off the plane and saw the filming of the attack, but now I envisioned the gut-wrenching reality of that terrible day. It felt as though ghosts of the war were still lingering.

Monday morning was disappointing. I discovered I had not been assigned to the computer facility but rather the communication hub of the base, a large and busy message center full of teletype and copying machines. Much of the classified information from the Vietnam War was processed here. I had wondered why some federal investigators had visited my parents and other family members several months ago, but I later found out it was because I needed a top secret security clearance for this job.

The war raged on. The year before had been the bloodiest one yet; men and women, many of them barely out of their teens, continued to die in Vietnam. The protests across the country grew larger and more frequent. I heard that one of the guys in my graduating class, the class clown, had been killed in combat. He lived on a farm outside of town, and I pictured the military chaplain arriving at his home to tell his family the heartbreaking news. I'm sure his death rocked our little town. It was hard to process the tragedy of people dying in war. To be tragically struck down on a faraway battlefield felt utterly senseless.

My thoughts once again turned to Tom. I was thankful he was safely home from the war. Although he had moved to Florida, he kept in touch with Kathy's husband. Both of them continued to struggle with alcohol addiction and the war-related emotional issues.

I also thought about the shocking stories from the women I had met over the past few years. Dad used to say, "Everybody has a story." I definitely had heard a lot of them since I left home. Some of the women had been sexually abused; some had alcoholic parents who fought all the time. One woman had lost both of her parents in a car accident. Still others had been the product of dysfunctional families where beatings were the tools of discipline. It was difficult for me to comprehend, and each time I listened, I felt a deeper sense of compassion. I realized that if there was such anger, lack of respect, and turmoil within a family unit, it was no wonder nations went to war.

As the war raged on and the protests continued, I prayed for peace and understanding. As a young active-duty member of the military, I also struggled to understand the protests. I believed they were acts of disloyalty.

Having a top secret security clearance sounded important, but I found the message center job to be boring. The teletype machines seldom stopped printing encrypted messages. We copied and stapled hundreds of them every week and then had to drive an ugly old truck to deliver them. Some of the messages went to the army base up in the mountains; others went to a marine base on the other side of the island. We delivered many of them to Pearl Harbor. I hated the job.

After several months of studying, I fulfilled the requirements to cross-train into the base computer center. I was relieved to be leaving the message center. Processing those messages was a constant reminder of the death and pain related to the war. Even though Tom was home, the thought of him continuing to suffer haunted me.

The base computer center was the central processing hub for the Pacific region. The Burroughs mainframe computer and its peripheral units filled an enormous room. After a few months, I was promoted to day-shift supervisor. I loved my job because it required my full attention. Like the IBM 1401 computer that I was exposed to in Florida, the Burroughs 3500 was a medium-sized second-generation computer. Processing speeds were faster, and the B3500 utilized a higher-level programming language (COBOL). The base operation was much larger and busier than the site in Florida. It was challenging to meet the day's processing requirements. Although I wanted to learn more about the programming language that made the mainframe computer work, I was satisfied for now. It was a genuine challenge to make the entire operation run efficiently, and it felt rewarding to finish each demanding shift.

After only a few weeks on the base, I met Mary, who was from Pennsylvania. Her room was only three doors down from mine. We were the same rank, from the same home state, and we were both rather quiet and reserved. Aside from that, we had little else in common. She had been abused as a child, and she joined the air force to get away from home. We had many long conversations where I just listened, and my heart hurt.

I wanted to "fix" Mary's life. I wanted her to know there were plenty of decent people in the world. Sometimes I felt embarrassed to talk about my childhood because it had been so loving; it had instilled confidence in me. Her low self-esteem was difficult for me to relate to. I hoped she would learn to see that we are each gifted in a unique way, and we each have value.

We took two trips together as our friendship deepened. On the first trip, we visited some of the other islands—Maui, Kauai, and Hawaii. All of the islands had been formed by volcanic rock, and each one had its own stunning beauty. However, by the time we were ready for our second trip, we both had what was known as "rock fever." That simply meant we needed to get off the islands and see something different!

We decided to fly to southern California to visit Disneyland. Neither one of us had ever flown on a military aircraft, so we decided to take a military *hop* from a naval air station not far from the base. As we boarded a KC-130 aircraft, we each received a boxed chicken lunch, and we were directed to a row of paratrooper seats that lined each side of the plane. The flight lasted about ten hours, and it was miserable. The seats were uncomfortable, the lunch was terrible, and the noise of the engines drowned out any attempt to talk.

Finally, we landed at the navy base in San Diego. Then we located a bus that went the remaining one hundred miles to Disneyland. It was almost twenty-four hours from the time we had left Hawaii until a crowded, dirty city bus dropped us off at the gates of Disneyland.

Once checked into a hotel, we rested for a few hours, and then we toured Disneyland. It was an unforgettable two days. We left our uniforms at the hotel and strolled through the park in civilian clothes. We weren't worried about having to salute any officers who walked by. We didn't have to go to the chow hall for lunch or dinner. Our carefree attitude was in direct contrast to the disciplined environment at the base. And there were no visible signs of an ocean! After such a grueling trip to get there, we set aside some of our spending money and happily paid for a commercial flight back to the island.

After receiving a promotion, I was excited to get approval for a loan at the base credit union. I bought a used 1968 MG Midget convertible for $1,800. It was the perfect car! Weekends were filled with trips around the island. Mary and I often met friends at our favorite snorkeling beaches and occasionally splurged for dinner at an upscale restaurant. But mostly, we went to mediocre bars where prices were low enough to stay and dance for hours.

Also, after I had bought my car, I didn't have to walk to work on base, and I was no longer subjected to the derogatory remarks hurled at most women. I was extremely proud of my uniform, but the guys on base were not shy about yelling out whatever they were thinking as they passed by. It had been the same situation at the Florida base. I resented their behavior there, and I resented it here.

While out dancing, there was seldom a time when I didn't hear "Unchained Melody." That song reminded me of the lighthearted high school years with Tom. A song that I once loved to hear now made me cry.

After a few months, I started dating a guy who lived on base. He was tall with blond hair, brown eyes, and a nice smile. He always took me to some of the nicer places at Waikiki Beach. I dressed up in the typical 1970s style of miniskirts, silky-looking blouses with long puffy sleeves, and platform shoes! His favorite place was a bar/lounge at the top of one of the tall hotels. We both loved to dance, but when "Unchained Melody" played, I did not dance with him. After he was transferred to a base in Texas, I never answered his letters.

My dormitory was only a block away from the men's transient barracks, and there was constant foot traffic in and out of the area. My most memorable experience there was the night I had an unexpected visitor. I was asleep in my bunk when I heard the floor creak. I opened my eyes and saw a man crawling across the floor toward my bed.

I don't know where I found the courage, but I asked him if he was okay. He crept over to the bed, put his hand on my back, and said he was lonely. I told him that I got lonely too, but I was going home soon. Then I asked him where he was from, and a conversation ensued. I listened while he told me about his assignment on a ship recently docked at Pearl Harbor. He hated the navy, and he missed home. After what felt like hours, I told him he would be in trouble if he was caught in our building. I offered to sneak him out the back door and meet him for lunch the next day, and he agreed! Once outside, we decided to meet at the back gate, and he left quietly.

After he left the dormitory, the reality of his visit set in, and I began to shake uncontrollably. I immediately notified the military police. I explained what had happened, and they instructed me to meet him as planned. I was scared to death, but I agreed. The next day, he was waiting at the gate. As I slowly approached him, the police rushed in and arrested him. A six-inch knife fell from underneath his shirt as he was being handcuffed.

I was shaken by this event, and it was frightening to think what could have happened to me. Fortunately, I had only one year of service left, and I was eligible to move off base. I was thankful to get away from the dormitory. I was weary of going to the base dining hall or to the kitchen downstairs to have dinner. Even though I had my own room, everyone in the building had to share one communal bathroom. But obviously, I was most relieved to get away from the transient area that was not well patrolled.

It was only natural that Mary and I become roommates, but the only place we could afford was a small studio apartment. The size wasn't important given its location downtown within walking distance to Waikiki Beach. I had recently traded my MG Midget in for a new Volkswagen Bug. Since there was only one parking space for us in the building garage and Mary also had a Volkswagen, we quickly learned how to squeeze both cars into one space.

When I drove to work each morning, I felt like a different person. Even though I was still in uniform, my life was not submerged in military surroundings. Dinner could be fixed in the privacy of our apartment, and I didn't have to wait in line to take a shower.

I enrolled at a local college downtown and attended a few classes in the evenings, but the learning process was far too slow. I preferred on-the-job training where you could quickly take what you learned and put it to practical use.

During this last year of duty, a new night-shift supervisor was transferred to the computer center from Japan. His name was Brian, and we instantly got along. During shift turnover in the mornings, he teased me if I had been unable to complete all the work that had been scheduled. Soon, we were competing to see which of our shifts produced the most work. It became a standing joke in the office, and surprisingly, everyone was happy when I beat him. I thought he was a friendly guy, and I didn't quite understand why they all wanted him to lose. He did, however, take our competition much more seriously than I did. When I asked him about it, he simply made some sort of joke, and we let it go. Soon after that, he said the hectic work schedule was getting to be too much, and he suggested that we stop competing.

Eventually, I took him to some favorite places like Pearl City Tavern, where delicious lobster dinners were a specialty. And dancing at some of the nightclubs in downtown Honolulu was always fun. He was very attentive and easy to talk to, and we enjoyed each other's company. We would sometimes double-date with Mary and Brian's best friend Cole, but Mary did not like Brian. She said she couldn't explain why, that she just "had a feeling" about him. When she asked why I always did whatever he wanted to do, I was somewhat confused. She worried that he had too much influence on my decisions. I didn't think that was true, so I didn't give it much thought. But regardless of what we all did together, they argued constantly.

As I approached the end of my tour of duty, I received a letter from the personnel department offering a generous bonus to reenlist for another four years. My two aunts had encouraged me to leave home, and my horizon had certainly widened just as they had predicted. I had grown in many ways, and with all the years of experience, my future looked promising as a *civilian*. If I reenlisted, I was sure I would have a successful career in the air force.

However, the bonus was not enticing. My decision to leave was based solely on the attitude of the majority of men stationed there. Their demeaning and undignified behavior toward their female peers was despicable. I was certain this would not be a choice that I would regret. I declined the offer.

Mary had also decided to not reenlist, and we began to plan our trip back to Pennsylvania. I kept my car and had it shipped to the port in Oakland, California. She sold hers and planned to help me drive. Cole lived in Ohio, and he asked if he could go with us since he couldn't afford to fly home. It only seemed fitting to let Brian come along since our relationship was getting serious. I thought it would be proper for him to meet my family, and it sounded like a fun trip. I could tell that Mary wasn't thrilled with the idea. The tension between the two of them remained, but I hoped a change of scenery with different things to see and do would help improve their relationship.

After we were honorably discharged, we boarded a flight to San Francisco. We spent two days sightseeing and then prepared for the long trip home. Brian and Cole met us in Oakland, and we were all literally stuffed into my Volkswagen with a mass of luggage piled on top. It was February, and we headed toward the east coast!

The trip was a disaster. I continued to be the peacemaker between Mary and Brian. They disagreed on which route to take. They argued about how to load the car each morning. They never agreed on where to stop for lunch. Then there was Cole who constantly complained about being cramped in the back seat.

It all came to an abrupt halt in Kansas City when Mary told me she could no longer tolerate all the arguing with Brian. She felt as though she was being "crowded out" of our friendship, and she wanted to fly home. I assured her that was not the case, and I tried desperately to convince her to stay with us. Certainly, since Brian had entered my life, she and I had spent less time together. I wondered if that was part of the problem, but I didn't ask. She was simply too hurt to listen, and she had obviously made up her mind days before.

During the night, I was unable to sleep, and I thought about some of the things she had said in the past. I wish we had talked more about her feelings, or had she just tried too many times, and I hadn't listened? Could it be true that Brian was controlling, or could she have just missed our time together more than I realized?

Tearfully, we said our goodbyes the next morning. We had spent three years together and had learned so much from each other. We were excited about making the trip home together, and we had anticipated it for months. Was this the death of our friendship? Would I see her again one day?

Our goodbye was too painful to even talk about it. I thought about Lois in Florida. She had mentored me. She was grounded and confident and focused. Because of her, my knowledge of technology had expanded to the point where I knew it was going to be my life's work. But even though I had spent time with her and her family, our focus was usually on my career.

It was different with Mary. Because of Lois, I was now the one who had become grounded and confident and focused. Mary was *lost* when I met her, adrift in her own self-worth. And now, three years later, I knew she felt that same way again as we parted.

Our time together ended so suddenly, and it was difficult to process. My loss was overwhelming. I had known Brian for less than a year. I fearfully wondered if I had missed some important signs. The fact that she was my best friend and Brian cared so little for her infuriated me, particularly after he appeared to be quite pleased to have her gone. We dropped Cole off in Ohio, and then we continued home in complete silence.

As I continued to wrestle with the circumstances of Mary's abrupt departure, Brian was polite and talkative, engaging in conversations with everyone at home. My family appeared to like him. Not surprisingly, I would learn later that he had been on his best behavior. He spent a week with us and then returned to Hawaii. We stayed in touch through letters and occasional phone calls.

There continued to be a lot of activity as friends and family stopped by to welcome me home, but the peacefulness I had always loved so much felt far too quiet. After two or three months of job searching, I was hired as a computer programmer for a pharmaceutical company in Rochester, New York. Even though I didn't have any programming experience, I was confident I could do the job if I was given a chance. Because of my experience and knowledge of technology, I was able to successfully bluff my way through the interview, and I was hired.

I committed to a start date, packed my paltry belongings, and moved into a furnished apartment a few miles from the office. The job provided some invaluable experience, but the adjustment of being alone and in a civilian environment was more difficult than I had anticipated. The office environment was very casual. People readily complained when they didn't like a new procedure or change. Working under pressure, like under a perceived unreasonable deadline, created a tense atmosphere. I was accustomed to a more disciplined and structured environment.

When Brian called and asked me to marry him and move back to Hawaii, I said yes. I quit my job after only a few months, and Brian flew back to Pennsylvania. We were married at the Presbyterian church where I had grown up and regularly attended. All of my family was present. A mutual friend and coworker of ours flew in from Hawaii for our wedding. Much to my surprise, Brian was annoyed with him for showing up unexpectedly. I thought his reaction was very odd since I was quite touched by our friend's thoughtfulness. Later that evening, Brian accused me of secretly inviting him. That absurd accusation hurled us into an argument on our wedding night.

The next day, we returned to Hawaii. We had not even left the airport before Brian accused me of flirting with a guy standing beside me while he went to get the car. While he raged all the way back to our apartment, my mind swirled as I tried to understand what was happening. I still wasn't able to make sense of the argument we had had the night before.

These irrational episodes of jealousy became an almost-daily occurrence. I was nervous any time a man walked by us on the street because Brian constantly watched to see if the guy smiled at me. If he did, I was accused of having a secret affair with him. When we rode in the car, I was afraid to look out the window at anyone passing by us. If I did, Brian wanted to know whom I was looking at and why. I was on edge all the time, and I felt myself succumbing to his control over me.

One evening during an argument, he punched me in my stomach. I ran to the bathroom and got sick. I locked myself in there until the apartment got quiet, and then I nervously peeked out and saw him sleeping on the couch. Our apartment building had twenty-five floors, and we lived on the seventeenth floor. I slipped out and climbed the stairs to the roof of the building.

I stood by the ledge overlooking what I had thought at one time was paradise. I screamed at the top of my lungs because I knew no one could hear me. I asked God what was happening, and *why* was it happening? I had done nothing to justify Brian's rage. I was not having an affair with the guy who smiled at us on the elevator. I did not know the guy who cut us off in traffic on the freeway. I was not flirting with the waiter at the restaurant who kept coming back to see if we needed anything. It was not my boyfriend who hung up when Brian answered the phone at home. I fearfully thought I had had a glimpse of insanity.

During another violent incident, I hit back...again and again. Eventually, through sheer exhaustion, I dropped on the couch, sobbing. Brian immediately started apologizing, as he always did, but I wanted to hear none of it. Once he fell asleep beside me, I got up, packed a small suitcase, and silently left, taking our only set of car keys. I drove to the airport, feeling frightened and confused, and I took the first flight to the mainland, a nonstop flight to Chicago. When I landed, I called my parents and asked them to pick me up in Pittsburgh in a few hours. I learned years later they were not surprised.

*****

This stop on my virtual tour caused me to look deep within myself. I could see now that I had married for all the wrong reasons. Although I was happy to learn a programming language at my job in Rochester, it was a strange and lonely environment that I had trouble adapting to. I was twenty-four years old when I had left the air force; in 1972, most women were married by that age. Apparently, I had thought it was just time for me to get married too.

I wondered about "that feeling" Mary had told me about Brian and how she thought he was controlling. I remembered how everyone at the office had been happy whenever I surpassed his workload accomplishments. How had I missed so many warning signs of potential trouble? I thought about his possessiveness. Anyone—male or female—was a threat to him and our relationship.

Mary and I had developed a deep and meaningful friendship. She had confided in me about her struggles with self-worth because of her childhood. I had used my loving childhood as an example of how people can truly love you. I felt ashamed that I had let Brian so intentionally damage our friendship.

I had met so many women, including Mary, who had joined the service to escape turmoil at home. Brian had left because he had gotten in trouble with his family for getting a girl pregnant. Even after being exposed to multiple horrendous stories, I continued to feel like I had not yet transcended my naive background. I was far too trusting.

Once again, I thought about Tom and the innocence of our years together in high school. He had gone off to a war that was difficult to comprehend. I had encountered a war of a different kind but one that was also beyond my comprehension. We had made our choices for different reasons, but the consequences had brought both of us pain and heartache. We had both lost that innocence.

During my three years in Hawaii, I had not gone home for a visit. The cost of a round-trip ticket from Honolulu to Pittsburgh had always been more than I could afford. I was unable to return for the funerals of my grandfather and my great-grandmother. I had never really been close to my grandfather because he was usually too busy to find time for any of us. I had visited my great-grandmother many times while growing up. By now, neither of them had been a part of my life for several years. The distance, both physical and emotional, gave me a sense of detachment, so my memories of them sufficed.

Since I had not attended their funerals, I did not have to see them and say goodbye. Once again, my thoughts of the fearful finality of death were easily and hurriedly pushed further down in my mind.

When I left Brian in Hawaii and flew home, I began to realize that I was not emotionally equipped to handle his frequent jealousy rampages. The fighting that had erupted on our wedding night was not just a one-time occurrence. I was not prepared for this new reality, nor was I prepared for what was still to come.

*****

Reflections

1. Were you ever involved in an unhealthy relationship where you failed to recognize the warning signs? What were the signs, and how did the relationship unfold?

   _____
   _____
   _____
   _____

2. We all make bad choices, but are they really mistakes if we learn something important from them? Describe a time when you thought you had made a mistake but it turned out to be a valuable lesson.

   _____
   _____
   _____
   _____

3. The loss of a friendship can literally cause our hearts to ache. There can be feelings of guilt, anger, sadness, and loneliness. We must allow ourselves time to grieve. How have you responded to a lost relationship?

   _____
   _____
   _____
   _____

CHAPTER 5

Another Choice

Shortly after I left Brian and returned home, we started communicating again. His tears and apologies sounded sincere, and I started questioning my decision to leave Hawaii so abruptly. Yet at the same time, I was frustrated and disappointed that our marriage was in trouble so soon. The intensity of his anger made me tremble, particularly since it was based on such outrageous claims. I was struggling to make sense of it all.

During this time, he received orders for a transfer to Dover AFB in Delaware, about a ten-hour drive from my hometown. Was this a sign that I should give in to his pleading and join him there?

Now that I was back home again, I reconsidered what a future here might be like for me. Once again, I thought that if I had followed my original plan of serving only four years in the air force, I would have been back here when Tom was discharged, and I would never have met Brian. How different things might have been.

Tom had eventually moved to Pittsburgh, where he worked for a large construction company, and here I was back home wondering what to do next. It was troubling to realize that all those independent decisions I had made over the past six years had simply brought me back to where I had started from.

I wrestled with whether to go back with Brian or create a new life for myself near my family. My mind told me that there could be danger ahead if I chose to rejoin him. My heart told me that he loved me and that he was, unlike me, tormented by an unhappy childhood. I decided to give our marriage another chance.

My parents were concerned about my decision because I had come home alone and so unexpectedly from Hawaii. I had never divulged any details about why I had left. I wasn't even sure I could describe the horror of the past several months.

Brian had all of our household goods shipped to Dover and then flew to Pittsburgh. I drove to the airport to pick him up, and it was an awkward reunion. When our eyes met as he came through the gate, he waved and had a big smile on his face. We hugged and kissed, and he promised only happy times ahead for us, but I felt tense. The last time I had seen him, his eyes were full of anger. My feelings of confusion and disappointment suddenly melted into a fearful sense of apprehension. I wondered if I had fooled myself into thinking life was going to be better.

After spending a few days with my parents, we drove to Dover to look for an apartment. It was late October, and the trees, bursting with vibrantly colored leaves, gave the small town a charming appeal. We drove down North State Street, where the trees along both sides were so large that they formed a natural canopy. It was gorgeous! Strangely, I felt this canopy wrapping me in a warm blanket of protection. I felt comforted, as though I had truly found a new home.

Some of the houses here were huge Victorians that reminded me of the ones back home. What quickly caught my attention, however, were the white wooden two-story houses with black shutters and lovely manicured lawns. I called them the father-knows-best houses, named after a favorite television show of the 1950s. The show was an idyllic presentation of family life. I could relate that show to my own family and the harmony that existed while I was growing up.

Right then, on that very first day in Dover on North State Street, I thought, *Someday, I'm going to live in one of these houses.* The strange part about that thought was that I did *not* think, *Someday, we are going to live in one of these houses.* That little subtlety didn't dawn on me until years later.

We had no trouble finding an apartment, and all of our household goods had already arrived at the base. We settled in and started exploring the town and the surrounding areas. The beaches were not what I was used to seeing. They were much smaller, and the Atlantic Ocean was a dull gray, not the multiple shades of blue as in the Gulf of Mexico or the Pacific Ocean. The Delaware landscape was extremely flat with endless fields that faded into the horizon.

Brian liked his job at the computer center on base. He said the people were friendly, and there was always plenty of work to keep him busy. Because he was basically a *loner*, and I wasn't working, we didn't make any friends. I enrolled in a ceramic class on the base and spent a part of most days out walking in the neighborhoods. Occasionally, we went to a movie or out to dinner. He was opposed to my getting a job right away, but after a few months, I was anxious to continue a technology career.

I saw an ad in the local newspaper for a computer programming position at a wholesale fabric company downtown. We had a few more arguments about my getting a job, and some of them were frightening. His unreasonable and unsubstantiated accusations left me speechless. My terrible memories of leaving Hawaii came flooding back. However, I was not going to let this opportunity go by without at least having an interview. Dover was a small town, and programming jobs were not plentiful.

I was only one of several applicants who applied for the job. The owner of the company conducted all interviews and said he would not make a decision for a few weeks. During this waiting period, life calmed down a bit with Brian, but I was becoming increasingly restless.

Weeks later, the owner called and offered me the job. I was initially surprised because I had had very little experience as a programmer. I had hardly dabbled in it while in the air force, had bluffed my way into my first job in Rochester, and had only stayed in that job for a few months. Now I was being offered one of only two full-time positions, and it required knowledge and experience in a language I had never heard of.

Confidence is a very powerful tool. It's not an emotion or a feeling; it's an act of *being*. Much like that job in Rochester, I accepted this position because I knew I could do it. When *you know that you know*, confidence abounds! I thought about how we had opened "The Spot." It had started with an idea and a decision to take a risk, and its success had instilled more confidence in me than I had originally thought. And I thought about Lois, my friend and mentor in Florida, who had instilled such confidence in me. Suddenly, I realized I was not surprised at the job offer after all.

I was, once again, deeply grateful for such an opportunity. I told the owner that I could start right away, so we agreed on the following Monday. I knew Brian would neither like the job offer nor the start date, but that was something he would have to accept.

I anxiously awaited Monday morning, knowing that his pent-up anger was the reason for his silent treatment over the weekend. It had been several months since we arrived in Dover. The absence of anything mentally challenging for me, coupled with our more-frequent arguing, had continued to strain our marriage.

The job was quite demanding, and there was a substantial backlog of programming requests. The company operated on a Memorex mainframe computer that was much smaller than the ones I was familiar with. Even though I had to learn an older programming language (RPG), my original excitement of those early days in the air force quickly returned. I felt as though I was back on track with a career.

The job turned out to be a blessing. Over the next several months, I was much happier at home. Although we still didn't socialize, the extra income allowed us to buy better-quality furniture and to save for a larger place to live. We had both grown tired of our small apartment. With less fighting, our life together became more enjoyable. We decided to start a family.

Our son Andy was born the following year. I had had no problems with my pregnancy, and more importantly, I felt no apprehension about taking care of a newborn baby. This was, no doubt, due in part to having had six younger siblings as I was growing up. Although the enormous new responsibilities and the upset in our normal daily routines were overwhelming at times, Andy brought an unparalleled degree of joy into my life. He was a happy baby, and we had lots of hugs and giggles. Watching him discover new things, learn new words, and seeing his personality develop were amazing experiences. Brian was also genuinely happy.

Life was going fairly well. My coworkers had surprised me with a baby shower that genuinely touched my heart. But even though I enjoyed the people at work, we still hadn't made any mutual friends.

After Andy was born, I took six weeks off from work. Brian requested to be assigned the night shift so he could be home with Andy after those six weeks ended, but that schedule proved too demanding for him. After working all night, he was only able to manage the morning routine; by afternoon, he was too tired to stay awake. I was concerned that Andy was not getting enough attention or playtime. We were able to maintain this schedule for only a month. In the meantime, my job was getting more demanding, and I started working overtime.

Fortunately, we found a woman who ran day care from her home. Judy watched one other child, and she had two small children of her own. I had such mixed feelings about leaving Andy with someone other than his father. But unless I quit my job, there was no other choice but to try day care. I was not quitting my job because I knew I was not a stay-at-home mother. I knew I would feel isolated with the lack of adult interaction, and I wanted to continue my exposure to a challenging career in technology. This was a source of continuous contention between Brian and me.

As it turned out, Judy was exceptional at caring for children, and we were very pleased with her. She was also willing to keep Andy for some additional hours on the evenings that I had to work overtime. Brian, on the other hand, was not so willing to accept my extra work hours. He started questioning why I had to work, what I was working on, and who I was working with. His subtle accusations, again, became unreasonable.

After picking Andy up at day care and going home, the evenings were filled with bitter arguments. There were many times when I took Andy into the bedroom and stayed there with him. Brian would often leave the house in a rage and not come back for hours. This usually meant he came home drunk. When that happened, I locked the bedroom door and held Andy while Brian pounded on it and bellowed out repulsive names at me. Even though Andy was too young to understand, I covered his little ears so he couldn't hear those names.

After each of Brian's outbursts, the house fell silent for days as we ignored each other. It was maddening, but that was the pattern that had developed. First, there was anger, outrageous accusations, and then fighting that was followed by silence, and eventually, his tears and apologies. The only difference now was that as things flared up, the incidents became more violent, especially when he had been drinking.

Finally, the special project at work ended, along with my overtime hours, and life calmed down again for a little while. Thoughts of separation occurred to me, but I did not make enough money to live on my own with a small child. That was not the only reason I didn't leave the marriage. It was also because of those tearful, apologetic sessions where Brian became remorseful, calmer, caring, and loving. I honestly felt sorry for the mental and emotional torture that I thought he went through. I thought if I tried harder to give him more attention, our life together would improve.

Over the next couple of years, there were continued bouts of rage followed by his tearful pleas for forgiveness. Of course, asking for forgiveness was part of Brian's manipulation. He was controlling me, and I didn't even realize it. Or perhaps I realized it, but I didn't want to acknowledge it. I had succumbed to his pattern of behavior.

I became pregnant again. With our combined incomes, we were able to rent a larger house and buy another used car. And the "Dr. Jekyll and Mr. Hyde" episodes became a way of life. More than once during an argument, I grabbed Andy and ran for the car. I usually got the car locked in time, and I would back out of the driveway with Brian pounding on the side window. My sister Kathy lived about one hundred miles away, in Lancaster, Pennsylvania, and I literally escaped to her home on several weekends. She knew we were having marital problems, but I was too ashamed to tell her how terrible it was.

Brian started living his own life, which included increased drinking and gambling. There was a casino and a harness racing track in town, and that was where he spent most of his time. Of course, the gambling habit impacted our financial situation. While paying bills one day, I noticed numerous checks were missing. and eventually discovered that Brian had cashed them at the racetrack. No wonder the bank was charging us for insufficient funds! I had to charge more and more of our purchases on credit cards. This only deepened our debt, and it made any chance of my leaving impossible.

Incredibly, as we were approaching bankruptcy, I was offered a better-paying programming job with the state of Delaware's technology department. I had put an application in at that office several weeks before because the fabric company that I worked for was in financial trouble. The owner had opened two new stores out of state, and it was more than his company could sustain.

It typically took a long time to get a position within state government. Many people applied for government jobs, not necessarily because of the salaries but because of the employee benefits and pension plans. I wasn't concerned about either of those factors when I had applied. I simply wanted a better income to help avoid bankruptcy.

I was deeply grateful when the state job became available. The fact that I was hired so soon after applying was close to a miracle. Just as everything appeared to be falling apart, I realized God had placed another opportunity in front of me. Much like finding a loving day care for Andy, this was a blessing that appeared in the midst of chaos.

I thought back to that terrible night on the roof of our apartment building in Hawaii when I had screamed and asked God what was happening. That had been a feeling of complete aloneness. But not long after that, I found the courage to leave Brian's abuse and had flown back home. Now as I looked back over the past couple years, I felt more hopeful. When I began to pay closer attention, I realized God had been—and still was—guiding and protecting me regardless of my choices. I had never been alone after all.

At my new job, I was assigned to a team of programmers who were all more experienced than me. The IBM 360 mainframe computer was several years old, but it far surpassed the processing capabilities of the mainframe I had worked on at the fabric company. The programming language was also different, but again, as with my two previous jobs, I learned the language in a relatively short period of time.

I loved the job, and at my sixth-month evaluation, my supervisor told me he was pleased with my work, and I was promoted. I went home that day feeling the best I had felt about myself in a very long time, and I went into labor that evening.

Our daughter Michelle was born the next morning, one month before Andy's third birthday. I was truly overwhelmed with joy at having these two little children. Our toy bin had been full of balls and cars and trucks. Now with a little girl, there were more pink clothes and toys in the house. Their presence far overshadowed the miserable aspects of my home situation. Once again, I took six weeks off work, and once again, since I was staying home with the kids, Brian was much calmer.

When I went back to work, life settled down. The kids consumed our time, and we shared most responsibilities. Judy agreed to watch both kids throughout the week. I dropped them off at her house each morning, and Brian picked them up after work. Their combined sweetness had, for now, transformed our tense and stress-filled life together into a more peaceful household.

We soon started looking for an even larger place to live and found a three-bedroom ranch-style house just a mile away. Brian used his veteran status to acquire a home loan with no down payment. With two little kids and a home we could call our own, I thought that as difficult as the years had been, maybe staying together was going to work out after all. I wondered, was giving him another chance the right thing to do, or was I simply fooling myself *again*?

*****

As I hovered over these few years, I was stunned at all that had happened. I felt such a range of emotions. Choices are not always obvious, nor are their consequences. Each choice we make adds information for our mind to hold and use as a filter for making future choices. We need this previous knowledge, and we need to pay attention to it to become more aware and make better choices in the future.

I looked closely at the choices I had made, both good and bad, and saw those years as learning some important life lessons. I felt humiliation because of the immaturity of my decision to get married. The staggering realization that I had married a man who was basically a stranger was difficult to accept.

I felt pain and confusion. I was so shocked and traumatized by Brian's jealous outbursts that I had lost my ability to think logically. I had no trouble solving complex problems on the computer, but I could not figure out what was happening in my own life. I had had no previous experience with such behavior, and even though I felt like I was in a tailspin, I had given him another chance.

I felt pure joy at the two little children who had brought such purpose into a world that literally made no sense to me. On many days when I had felt so helpless, their innocence had given me the courage to keep going.

I felt naive and discouraged. Why had I put up with an abusive environment for so long?

I felt grateful for the opportunities to work and expand my career.

I felt humbled. Under the circumstances, I had tried to do the best that I could. Although still confused and unable to fully recognize what was going on, I had grown in many ways.

Most importantly, I had become more aware of God's presence even during the most difficult times. My prayers consisted more of thankfulness than of asking for help.

*****

Reflections

1. Think of a decision you have made and then changed your mind. Was that subsequent decision based upon facts or feelings? Do you wish you had not changed your mind?

   _____
   _____
   _____
   _____

2. Are you a risk-taker, or do you stay in your comfort zone? Describe a missed opportunity when you wished you had taken a chance.

   _____
   _____
   _____
   _____

3. A form of grief can be the loss of childhood innocence. Name an event you experienced that you felt took away your innocence?

   _____
   _____
   _____
   _____

CHAPTER 6

A Death without Grief

Shortly after Michelle was born, we decided to take a vacation. In the five years that we had been married, Brian and I had only taken one vacation, and that was a nightmarish experience. We had flown to Miami to spend a week at the beach. Each day, I was accused of flirting with someone—the desk clerk, the waiter, the bartender, the lifeguard, the dad walking along the water with his little girl. It was perverse. There was not a single day that we didn't fight, and we fought with both words and fists.

As a result of that vacation, I was hesitant to agree to another one, but since we would rent a small cottage on a quiet lake in Southwestern New York, I thought perhaps things would be better than they had been in Miami. There would be no evenings out because we would have Andy and Michelle with us. There would be family who would come for a visit. I would have to return to work soon and reasoned that a change of scenery might do us both good, so off we went.

The cottage was lovely, and it was located within fifty yards of the lake. The weather was warm and sunny every day. My parents and some of my siblings came for a day since we were less than one hundred miles from my hometown. Andy loved splashing in the water and all of the attention from family members. Michelle was an infant, and she brought smiles to everyone as Mom and my sisters took turns holding her. It was a relaxed environment, and Brian and I did not argue about anything.

All in all, it was enjoyable, except for a crippling rash that developed on my arms and legs shortly before we left for home. My joints became inflamed, and I could hardly walk. I saw a doctor and got antibiotics for ten days. It was a rather bizarre incident, and it disappeared almost as quickly as it came. I suspected that it was related to the stress of going back home.

Once back in Dover, we spent all our time at our new home. We couldn't afford the furniture that we wanted, but we made a budget, and we agreed to work toward getting back on our feet financially. Brian decided to retire from the air force within the next two or three years. It felt as though we had some tangible goals to aim for.

Upon returning to work, my days were busy coding complex systems that required working with many team members. It was a much-more-social environment than I was accustomed to working in. I was the junior programmer on the team. During our weekly team meetings, I was quiet and tried to absorb as much as I could about the various programming standards and office procedures.

With each assignment, I flowcharted and coded numerous business processes at my desk, and then I went to the keypunch room to punch the code into IBM cards. I often volunteered to keypunch programs for other team members after I saw them struggling to finish. This was a good way to meet people, and I quickly felt comfortable in the new job.

My thoughts turned back to the keypunch job that had been my first assignment in the military. That job had become the cornerstone of my career. The series of life events that had transpired since then had led me to this new job. Opportunities were offered. Choices were made. I suddenly felt overwhelmed with a deep sense of gratitude. Even as my chaotic life consumed my thoughts, I knew God had always been with me.

There were regular fifteen-minute breaks at work in the morning and afternoon when our team went down the hall to a room filled with vending machines. It was a relaxing time to talk about our individual lives outside the office. They were a friendly group, and I was delighted with the interaction. We had been in Dover for almost six years, and we had still not made any mutual friends. We had only recently and briefly met our new neighbors.

My first real social event was the office Christmas party. It was Friday, and we closed the office early and went to a local restaurant for dinner. There was a bar, a large dance floor, and the music was loud and upbeat. Everyone was relaxed and in a good mood, and it was truly a pleasant evening out. When the disc jockey played "Unchained Melody," my conversation stopped, and my mind wandered back to those happier years with Tom.

I had insisted that Brian watch the kids so that I could go to the party. I explained how it was a new job and that it was important for me to build relationships with the people I worked with. As the evening went on, I was enjoying myself so much that I lost track of the time. When I realized how late it was, I rushed home. I was in such a good frame of mind that I didn't consider Brian might be upset.

The enjoyable evening came to a screeching halt as soon as I came through the front door. The living room exploded into a firestorm of accusations, insults, and vulgarities. I had no chance to say a word in my defense before the first slap came to the side of my head…and then another one, and then I hit back as hard as I could. I ran into the bedroom, locked the door, and sobbed uncontrollably as Brian pounded his fists on the door.

When I heard the baby crying, I unlocked the door, looked directly at him, and dared him to hit me again. He was seething, but he just stared at me. I went into the kids' room and stayed there for the rest of the night.

Thankfully, it was the weekend, so I didn't have to go to work. I didn't know if I was sore from being hit or from hitting, but it didn't matter. I was grateful that Brian was not home when I woke up. I showered and had a quiet day with the kids, holding them tightly with intermittent tears as I desperately tried to determine what to do next.

We were sitting outside on the front steps after dinner when Brian finally came home. I braced myself, but I knew he would not hurt the kids. He just walked by us and went into the house. There were no words exchanged while I got the kids ready for bed, and I spent another night in their room.

The next day was predictably full of tears. I don't know who cried more, but we cried for different reasons. Brian claimed he was sorry and apologized for his anger and his behavior. I cried because I felt trapped in a hopeless situation.

The next several days were tense. I felt that if I let my guard down, there would be another outburst of some sort. I kept a low profile, doing and saying only enough to keep our home life civil. By now, I knew the routine.

Weeks faded into months, and months faded into years. The days at work were very busy, and the kids and household chores consumed the evenings. There were frequent stretches of arguing followed by days of silence. There were also pleasant days. Andy and Michelle oftentimes broke the silence with their silliness. Their laughter was infectious. We were both captivated as they learned new colors and words. It felt like there was always a *first* happening—first tooth, first crawl, first step. Andy had as assortment of balls and loved to run around the backyard. When Michelle took her first steps, the house exploded with applause!

We had two cars, and by now, I was aware that Brian was tracking the miles on each one. No matter which car I drove, when the miles driven didn't appear to equal the distance of my planned errands, an argument erupted. I was accused of meeting someone for some sordid reason. But something different was happening now. After I finished my errands, I sometimes went for longer rides just to put more miles on the car and raise his suspicions.

Regardless of the intensity of the confrontation, I was feeling more emboldened. I became more aware of how Brian manipulated me. His jealous behavior on our wedding day had thrown me for a loop. I had been unable to comprehend it, and it had eventually turned me into a frightened, timid person. But now I wanted my self-esteem back.

It especially bothered Brian when I left for a weekend. Many weekends, I packed a bag and took the kids to visit Kathy. Her children were about the same ages as Andy and Michelle, so they had fun times with each other in a normal family environment. Kathy was a good listener, and the time away gave me a chance to relax a little. I never described all the horrendous details of the fighting at home to her. Always on the drive back to Dover, I felt myself getting tense, and I tried to prepare for what might be waiting for me.

One summer, we drove to Maine to visit Brian's family. This was the first time I had met them, and we had been married for five years. None of them had traveled to my hometown to attend our wedding.

We stayed at his brother's camp on a beautiful lake. His siblings had children too, and we all enjoyed watching them get acquainted. I wanted to know more about his childhood, but I was too embarrassed to ask. Instead, it was a typical family reunion, and the return trip home was uneventful.

We made several trips back to my hometown over the years. They were always busy trips because I had so many relatives to visit. If Brian and I went to the grocery store and I happened to run into an old classmate, there was a subsequent argument with the typical accusations. The arguments weren't as forceful as they were at our own home because too many family members were present now. Still, my parents heard our loud voices late at night. I was sure they wanted to know what was going on, but I never gave them the opportunity to ask. I was too ashamed to let them know how unhappy I was.

When it was time for Andy to go to kindergarten, we needed to find new day care for both children. Again, we found a woman who had day care at her home, and it was a perfect arrangement. She lived directly across from the school and only four blocks from our home. She had one daughter, who was three years older than Andy, and both the kids loved her. In the midst of all the emotional turmoil at home, I was grateful for a calmer place for the kids to stay. Once again, I was acutely aware of God's presence. The peace I felt with the care given to the kids allowed me to become stronger in the more painful areas of my life. I began to think more clearly and became increasingly more aware of Brian's controlling behavior.

Work was going exceptionally well, and I was given greater responsibilities that resulted in promotions. I was eventually assigned as a project leader for a multiyear criminal justice project. That meant I was out of the office quite often while I met with the client at state police headquarters. I knew that it bothered Brian because of the insinuations he muttered under his breath when I got home. For the most part, I did not respond to his accusations. I had learned to respond only to fights worth fighting. Those were the fights where I had to physically defend myself.

The client that I was working with was a woman ten years younger than me. Her name was Terri, and she lived only a few blocks from our home. We were very different people. She was an extrovert; I was an introvert. She was single; I was married with children. Her favorite music involved fiddles; I loved violins. She had dozens of friends; I had almost none. I once told her she was "an inch deep and a mile wide." She laughed when I explained that if I had that many friends, I couldn't give the attention they deserved as my friend. She just laughed again and told me that my personality was too intense.

I was surprised by Terri's statement, but it was true. I had known plenty of acquaintances over the years, but a true and deep friendship, to me, deserved a degree of devoted time and attention. For all the years I had been in the military, I really only had one friend at each base—Lois in Florida and Mary in Hawaii. Lois was single, and she had been faced daily with the health challenges of her mother and sister at home. Mary was single, and she had left home because of abuse problems. Now here was Terri, single and one of the happiest people I had ever met. It felt strange to be around someone who appeared to not have a care in the world.

One day early in our friendship, Terri called me in the morning and said, "Let's go to Great Adventure!" That was a large amusement park in New Jersey about a hundred miles north of Dover. I had heard about it, but I didn't know anyone who had been there. Surprisingly, Brian agreed to watch the kids for a day, so I was excited about getting away to see a new place, and I thought it would be a great time for Terri and me to get to know each other a little better.

After driving for an hour or so, we got off the turnpike exit. It was almost noon, and we were getting hungry. There was a bar right near the exit ramp. Terri drove into the parking lot, and we went inside to check out their lunch menu. It wasn't a very large place, but it looked like it might have been a favorite hangout with the locals. There were a couple of dartboards nailed to the wall, and a long shuffleboard table game was in the back of the room.

Terri was very outgoing, so it only took her a few minutes to get a conversation started with some people at the bar. Once we ordered our food and a beer, they invited us to play darts with them. We never did make it to Great Adventure! We stayed there for several hours and had a fantastic time playing games. This was so out of character for me, but Terri was right at home, and her enthusiasm was infectious! I never told Brian that we didn't go to the park, and Terri and I laughed about it for years!

Brian was ready to retire from the air force and had started looking for a job in Dover. After several weeks, he was offered a position as night-shift supervisor of computer operations at a large business in town. Although he had been stationed at Dover AFB for ten years, he had never introduced me to any of his friends.

Terri and I spent a lot of time together, both working on the project and talking personally as friends. Because she was single, most of her friends were single. That was a good reason for Brian to continue to hurl his irrational accusations. Many times, while I was on the phone with Terri, she heard him yelling at me. One day, she asked me if he had ever hit me. My silence said it all. It soon became obvious that Brian didn't like Terri, and Terri definitely did not like Brian.

Terri and I started walking after work and talked about how to proceed with the project. If we didn't go walking, we talked on the phone and waded through the countless details of the new system, which tracked all crimes in the state and sent regular statistical updates to the FBI. Since the crime statistics were released to news agencies, system results were under meticulous scrutiny by both her commander and the CEO of my department. We knew how important it was to have a successful project, and it was going to require a great deal of time from both of us.

We also walked on Saturday mornings when Brian was home with the kids. We often went by a large house on a corner lot downtown where a long, high fence was being built. It became a constant topic of conversation since we compared its construction to the methodical construction of our new computer system.

When construction suddenly stopped, the bare wood was exposed to the weather without any paint or primer. Terri said this was a costly project mistake. I laughed at that because she had quickly grasped the mechanics of building a new system. She had common sense and an aptitude for understanding project challenges and pitfalls.

I had thought a lot about what Terri had said about my having an intense personality. I wanted to show her that I could, in fact, be just as unstructured and spontaneous as she was! One Saturday after our walk, I went back to that house and knocked on the door. I assumed the lady who opened it was the homeowner. I told her how my friend and I admired her fence, but we wondered why it wasn't being painted. She looked at me strangely, and I explained that we often walked around town, and we had watched it being built for the past several months. The fence was six feet high and constructed with hundreds of one-inch square stakes. She said she had been unable to find anyone interested in such a tedious paint job.

My heart started racing, and I was sure she could hear it pounding through the screen door. I immediately told her that we would be happy to paint it. To my delight she said okay, and we worked out a few details. When I got back to Terri's house and told her what I had done, she was speechless for a moment, and then we both laughed hysterically at such an impulsive idea.

Since we both had full-time jobs, we could only paint during the evenings and on weekends. I was amazed when Brian agreed to watch the kids, but his willingness didn't last long. Sometimes I dropped the kids off at their day care home.

Once we got enough money from the homeowner to buy brushes, paint, and primer, we started the job. It was March, and it was cold and windy. Each weekend, we painted for hours. Terri painted on one side of the fence, and I painted on the other side. We initially talked about our project, but the conversations soon turned to more personal topics.

Terri's parents had separated years before, and she lived with her mother. One of her goals was to save enough money to buy her own home. She had been a waitress before getting her current job at state police headquarters, and given her low salary, it would be years before she could achieve that goal.

I told her about growing up in a small town with a big family, and she always asked a lot of questions, like what was it like with so many kids in the family? What did we do for fun since our school classes were so small? Did I have to share a bedroom with my sisters?

I told her about the time when my sister, friend, and I had set up a new place to hang out one summer when we had been bored. Then I asked her if she had ever thought about opening a business of some type. She just laughed and said she didn't have any talent, so no, she had never considered it.

We painted as many evenings and weekends as possible while the fighting at home continued. As always, each fight ended with a few days of silence, and then Brian willingly watched the kids as part of his "apologizing routine." It didn't take Terri long to learn his predictable behavior.

Throughout all the long months of painting, an important transformation was underway. It wasn't the weather, although it changed from gusty snow flurries to oppressive humidity. It wasn't the freshly painted coarse wooden fence that actually added charm to the owner's home. It wasn't even the new acquaintances we made as many strangers stopped by to ask how we were doing.

The transformation happened as we stood on either side of the fence, painting and talking through those jagged wooden stakes for endless, aching hours. Our friendship reached a depth that neither one of us had experienced before.

I learned that Terri had been restless and bored with her job until just recently when she had been assigned to the FBI project. She learned more about my life at home and how I struggled to make sense of it all. Our mantra was, "Never face the facts!" In addition to giving us a lot of laughs, it was an inspiring message that encouraged us to take risks. It helped us believe better days were ahead for both of us.

Her eagerness to learn all that she could about computer design and programming reminded me of myself years earlier. Although I didn't mention it while we painted, in the back of my mind was a lingering thought of starting a business of my own and asking Terri to join me.

Finally, we finished the job in mid-July, working in the oppressive heat and slapping mosquitoes with our paint brushes. After the fence was painted, Terri came over to my home more often. I didn't realize it then, but she was on a mission to see just how Brian behaved. It didn't take long. Brian was not shy about showing his contempt for her, nor did he withhold any innuendos about what he thought we were doing. One day, he told her that he knew all about the bar we had stopped at while we were out walking downtown. Terri was stunned and denied it, but Brian angrily told her to quit defending me. Even though I was embarrassed to have her witness such behavior, I was glad someone else actually saw it.

Brian did not like civilian life, and he started drinking more. Terri was leaving one evening just as he came home, loud, obnoxious, and full of crude name-calling. She was again appalled, but this time, she was also frightened. She told me I needed to get away from him before something terrible happened. I knew she was right. I had been having more thoughts of leaving, and a voice deep within my soul was compelling me to take action.

The fights erupted more frequently, but I was no longer intimidated by his vocal outbursts and assaults. I stood up for myself and fought back with a vengeance. He had as many bruises as I did. One night, I told him I was leaving him. I was no longer going to live in fear, and he was not going to control me. He was livid. This time after the fight ended, there were no tears or apologies. He had reached a new level of anger and suspicion, and I had reached a new level of defiance.

Terri continued to plead with me to "get out." Brian knew I lacked the courage. Where would I go? How could I live on just my income with two little kids? I had let him create a situation that was seemingly impossible to escape from.

Our home became a living hell, and I was worried about the kids. Andy was almost ten years old, and Michelle was seven. I tried to shield them from the arguments, but it wasn't always possible. When an argument got nasty, I took them outside or into another room, but Brian sometimes followed us and bellowed out his delusions. He never physically harmed the kids, but I was still worried how the intense arguing might affect them emotionally.

Several weeks earlier, during a more pleasant time, Brian had agreed to become more sociable and join my office bowling team. Neither one of us had bowled in years, and I thought it might be fun if he actually met some of my team members. I had hoped he could see for himself that I was only friends with them. He appeared to enjoy it at first, but the more fun I had, the less he liked it. Because of our arguing, we had sporadically missed some weeks during the bowling season. Each time I had to make up some sort of excuse for our absence.

Our last night of bowling was another tense outing. On our way home, Brian suddenly asked me how long I had been having an affair with one of the guys on the team. I looked at him, shook my head, and told him he was crazy. The next thing I knew, I was hit hard in the face. I was stunned. All I could taste was blood. I hurt so bad, I couldn't even scream. I just leaned over on the side window and cried. When we got home, he tried to help me out of the car, but I pushed him away. Still shaking and crying, I got in the house by myself, and I went straight to the bathroom.

The person I saw in the mirror was not me. She was a bruised and battered woman who was letting her life slip away. She was a mother who was faced with protecting her children. She was not the confident, independent girl who had been so excited to experience all the world had to offer. I was overcome with a deep, deep sadness.

It was a painful night on so many levels. My front teeth were slanted back into my mouth. It was difficult to talk, but I managed to call my dentist in the morning. When I told him I had been in an accident, he said to come right into the office. I drove myself even though I could barely see through my swollen eyes.

When I told the dentist that I had hit the dashboard of the car during a sudden stop, I knew he didn't believe me. I didn't care. I had both front teeth capped. The dental work was lengthy and painful, and I missed several days of work. For me, this was the beginning of the end. I was no longer concerned about how I would support myself and my children. Terri had constantly said everything would work out okay once I got away. She reminded me of the courage she knew I had. I realized then that somehow I had to find it again. It was heart-wrenching to know that I had let Brian make me feel so powerless for so long.

Brian also knew there was no going back this time. Over the next several days, he simply left me alone. Once my face swelling went down and I could talk clearly, I told him I wanted a divorce. He didn't try to talk me out of it. The divorce proceedings were simple and quick. We had qualified for a $25,000 home equity loan, and Brian agreed to relinquish his share of the house for that amount. Although we agreed to joint custody with the kids, I knew he had no intention of staying in town.

I wanted nothing from him, but Terri convinced me that I needed money for the kids, so I agreed to accept $250 a month for child support. The divorce papers were signed, and I wrote him a check for $25,000. He walked out on his job. He said goodbye to the kids, and he left town.

*****

As I looked upon this part of my virtual tour, I realized there was a great deal that I did not remember. I had been married for twelve years, but there were long periods of that time that had completely evaporated from my memory. What I did remember was feeling sorry for Brian. I thought I could change him, make him feel loved. I thought the kids needed their father. I was afraid of not being able to support them on my own. I had all kinds of excuses for staying, but once the marriage was over, I had no doubts that I had done everything I could have done to save it. And I had two precious children.

My marriage was dead. When it ended, I felt no grief, no loss. The finality of this death did not bother me. I didn't think about that vast emptiness that I had feared all of my life. I knew life would be difficult, but I didn't feel as though I needed the comforting from friends and family that is so often needed after a death. I didn't think the world should stop spinning while I mourned. Yes, the kids had lost their father, but I had lost crying myself to sleep at nights, trembling behind locked doors, and futilely defending myself against senseless lies and terrifying intimidation. I felt no grief.

I hovered here for a very long time. Initially, I didn't want to relive this part of my life, but I was glad I did. It brought tears and painful memories, but it helped me walk through a door that I thought I had already passed through. Seeing the experience written down on paper has, not surprisingly, made it more real. I actually lived through it. I am a stronger person with more empathy not only for the abused but also for the abuser. I'm sorry my children don't remember more about their childhood, but I understand why, and it's actually a blessing.

All experiences are temporary. We have the ability to give them a reason for happening. So even though my encounter of abuse was shocking to my mind and body, perhaps it was necessary for my soul. The empathy I learned by living through it has been a gift to others over the years.

God gave us free will. Brian chose, for whatever reason, to be an abuser, to strike out at me for his own reasons. Initially, I chose to stay, and then I chose to leave. We each have the choice to move forward…or not.

*****

Reflections

1. Fear of another person can render us powerless. We become a victim and lose our self-worth, but this is a voluntary choice. Can you describe a time when you overcame the fear of someone or something? Why did you choose to no longer be a victim?

   _____
   _____
   _____
   _____

2. Do you trust in a power that transcends your everyday reality? What helps you get through difficult times?

   _____
   _____
   _____
   _____

3. Have you ever found yourself arguing with reality, failing to admit what seemed obvious to others? Why do you think you let that happen?

   _____
   _____
   _____
   _____

CHAPTER 7

Good and Plenty

My divorce brought me peace—quiet, calming, reassuring, blessed peace. There was no longer a reason to feel on edge or wonder what the next hour or day might be like. When I locked the front door of my home, I felt safe. *My* home.

Andy and Michelle were doing fine. Strangely, they had not asked for Daddy. My days were filled with working, housekeeping, errands, and the kids' activities—school, Scouts, and sports. A single mom can surely say, "The buck stops here."

Brian and I had closed all joint accounts before he left. When my new checks arrived in the mail, it was odd to see only my name printed on them. This gave me confidence. I knew I faced a mountain of bills, which now included the recent home equity monthly payment, and they exceeded my income, but I was confident and motivated.

In order to pay the bills and maintain the household, I used cash advance checks from one credit card to pay another one and, all the while, putting additional purchases on the cards. It was a vicious circle of unending debt, but it was the only way I could survive. I was grateful Terri had convinced me to accept monthly child support payments from Brian.

There is no way to anticipate some of the difficulties in life. I certainly never expected to be in such dire financial trouble, especially as the result of an abusive marriage that had shaken me to my core. Regardless, I knew things could be much worse. I was blessed with two precious children, a roof over our heads, a car for transportation, and a decent-paying job.

I was also blessed with a true friend in Terri. For most of my marriage, I didn't have any real friends to talk to, only occasional acquaintances for casual conversation. I had let Brian's jealousy prevent me from having any close relationships. But after meeting Terri, her larger-than-life personality and her genuine concern for my well-being left no room to shy away and remain under his control.

God had seen me through some tough times. It wasn't a coincidence that the kids had always had loving, caring women for day care. It wasn't a coincidence that I had been hired for a better-paying job just as Brian's gambling propelled us deep into debt. It wasn't a coincidence that Terri had appeared in my life just when I needed her most.

Trusting God with the details of life meant that I didn't need to fear what was ahead. I believed God would equip me with the guidance and the strength to get through any situation. These were worrisome days indeed, but I felt a sense of peace that I could not describe. I moved in and out of the weeks and months with a renewed sense of independence.

I had found the courage that I thought I had lost and knew it was important to keep a positive attitude. My marriage had taught me some fundamental lessons. As long as my choice was to stay in the abusive marriage, I continued to tolerate and enable Brian's behavior. When my choice was to get out of it, everything changed.

I had also gained a deeper sense of empathy for why women stay in an abusive marriage. There was the financial worry of not being able to support myself and two children. As absurd as it might sound, there was an overarching desire to *help* Brian, to let him know that he was loved. There was the potential embarrassment and shame, as no one in my family had ever been divorced.

My days at work were extremely busy as Terri and I immersed ourselves in the FBI project. The more system requirements we uncovered, the more complicated the process became. Terri had an optimistic attitude and a level of energy and enthusiasm that were both rare and contagious. We tackled project problems with an approach that often resulted in sidesplitting laughter.

Terri's job was to understand the function of the system, and my job was to translate those functions into program code. Defining and documenting new system requirements can be a frustrating and tedious job. Subsequently, translating those requirements into code—and then testing the logic—is where results are confirmed as being correct or not. As we tested the system, there were several times when the expected result was incorrect. Instead of getting frustrated, we were usually able to find something humorous in how we had misinterpreted the requirement so differently. Either she hadn't fully understood it, or what I had heard is not what she had said. This approach helped to relieve the usual tension when implementing a new system!

During the first year of my divorce, I often felt overwhelmed with the responsibilities of single parenthood. Terri came to my home more often so we could work after hours on the system. Our walking days were virtually eliminated since I could not leave the kids alone. My once-frequent trips to visit my sister Kathy were also reduced because of my financial situation.

More and more, as time went by, Terri became an integral part of our family. The kids readily accepted her as she spent more time with all of us. They learned what friendship was all about simply by being exposed to her.

When I could work it into my budget, the kids and I took an occasional trip back to my hometown. Just as I had done when I was young, they spent two weeks during the summers with their grandparents. Over the years, I lost both of my grandmothers and my dear aunt Mamie. They had all been such an important part of my childhood, and I had visited them as often as possible. They always talked about those summers when my siblings and I stayed with them—the card games at the kitchen table, the smell of sugar cookies, the giggles. They had all been so proud of me for striking out on my own. With each loss, my heart was wounded, and I felt a deep sadness.

The FBI project was eventually completed, and Terri and I were grateful for a successful implementation. Our work together had been more than just another computer project. The experience resulted in an appreciation of how to persevere through difficult times. It was a profound adventure in developing a more in-depth understanding that true friendship comes from listening, patience, acceptance...and yes, laughter.

With the completion of the project, I was put in charge of managing the integration of multiple systems where similar business processes could be combined. The buzzword in the business world was "business process reengineering."

In the early days of computer programming, systems were designed so that more work could be accomplished in a shorter period of time. That was the whole concept of automation. As technology progressed, it became glaringly apparent that there were thousands of *inefficient* business processes that had simply been made faster!

It was not only an exciting new job; it was another profound occurrence of God's intervention. As a single mother with two small children, I had been struggling with making ends meet; my expenses exceeded my income, and my boss Rich was aware of my circumstances.

Rich actually created this new management job. It came with a substantial salary that allowed me to begin to see daylight again. With a little time and careful planning, my financial situation improved significantly. It was extremely gratifying but not surprising that once again, what had initially felt like an impossible situation had worked out.

Terri said the months of intense problem-solving and testing during the FBI project had put her senses on "high alert." After the implementation, she was back to her routine office work, which bored her. She called one day to complain. I heard the frustration in her voice, and I glibly said, "Well, why don't you just quit?"

She laughed and hung up.

When we painted that fence, I had wondered what it might be like if we became partners and started a computer software business. During the FBI project, she showed an intense desire to learn programming. As time permitted, I taught her various aspects of analyzing and coding. I knew she had an aptitude for it, and I encouraged her to pursue a career in technology.

When I called her a few days later at her office to discuss a system update, the receptionist said, "Oh, she quit."

"What?" I exclaimed.

"Yes, Terri resigned. Yesterday was her last day here. We are really going to miss her."

I hung up the phone in disbelief.

When I called Terri at home, she answered the phone and chuckled as soon as I said hello. "What are you doing at home?" I asked.

She calmly said, "You told me to quit, so I did."

I was shocked at her statement! I had been so grateful for how she had helped me find the strength to leave my abusive marriage. We had walked and talked and laughed for hours on end, yet I had never considered that she, too, was listening and learning and trusting. It was a moment of deep fulfillment.

It was 1986, and the explosion of the personal computer was well underway. New programming languages were widely available for businesses, and individuals could now write customized stand-alone systems.

Incredibly, it was now time to have that discussion about opening a programming business. I couldn't believe how the pieces began to fall into place. At first, Terri laughed when I told her we should become partners. After she realized that I wasn't kidding, we decided to invest in the purchase of an IBM XT personal computer and learn to program one of the newer languages, dBase.

Since I was still working full-time, it was up to her to learn dBase. Once she was confident with writing programs, we contacted a mutual friend who owned a restaurant. We explained how his business could run more efficiently by automating the tedious manual bookkeeping processes. Additionally, the system could be customized specifically for his business. He agreed to purchase a personal computer, and our business was launched!

Soon, we were writing customized systems for gas stations, bowling alleys, colleges, tree farms, crop dusters, insurance agents, and city, county, and state agencies. Terri was inundated with work, and I resigned from state government within a few months.

Our business grew by leaps and bounds. Our only advertising was through word of mouth, and we both worked from our homes, so we had no overhead. Since Terri had become so involved with our local clients, I did most of the necessary traveling. The kids were teenagers now, so they could be left alone for a few hours. I never scheduled any overnight trips even though some clients were in a different state.

One system required many trips to Maryland. The owner, Frank, was an older man who was a wholesale textile dealer. He had a small office in a dilapidated part of Baltimore. Although his business was extremely successful, he lived a very unassuming life. He drove an older model car, and he always wore a wrinkled shirt. When I first met him, I told Terri that I wished we could afford to write his system at no cost. Of course, she laughed!

Frank and I talked for many hours about the events in our lives. He had grown up being very trusting of people, but he was not afraid to take risks. He had started his business on an impulse, and he took great delight in his employees as his company continued to thrive. He was fascinated that I had joined the military, and he asked many questions about my experiences.

The drive to Baltimore took two hours. On the way to his office, my thoughts were always crowded with his technology needs. But during the late-night drives home, I thought about his humble beginnings, and I saw many parallels in my own life. The traveling and system work were grueling, but I was deeply grateful for the opportunity to have met this man.

Frank was just one example of the relationships we built over the years. Our lives were enriched by everyone we met. Most of them were ordinary people who had either created a small business or were operating a business that had been in the family for years.

It was gratifying to feel the confidence our customers had in us as they turned over their entire operation for us to automate. As we learned the intricacies of their individual businesses, we also learned more about life in general through the stories they shared. They ranged from joyous events—such as new babies, weddings, graduations—to tragic accidents, terminal illnesses, and deaths of beloved friends and family.

During one of our busiest years, I was offered a position again with state government, but this time, it was as a consultant for several mainframe computer implementations. This added a new dimension to our business, and although it was very lucrative, it put a strain on the number of small businesses we could support. We struggled to keep up with our workload.

We had been in business for nearly ten years when the technology industry began to produce low-cost generic off-the-shelf systems that fit the needs of most businesses. We saw the handwriting on the wall. We knew that the niche we had found for writing customized systems would not last much longer.

*****

Hovering over this time in my life made me smile. These were good years. There were certainly initial struggles as a single mother. I worked long and arduous hours, both at home and at work. The kids were happy and doing well. And with a caring and compassionate boss who offered me a new career opportunity, I eventually found myself on a solid financial foundation.

Not only did Terri and I start a business that thrived, our friendship also deepened. It had been the laughter that Terri and I shared that had initially sparked our friendship. Although life at home had been stressful, our laughter made my heart joyful and gave me hope. It was good for my soul. It had a healing power, and it had brought a sense of balance that allowed me to begin to see more clearly what had been happening in my marriage.

Terri and I both purchased homes in downtown Dover only a few blocks apart. My new home was on North State Street, the same street I vowed to live on when I had first arrived in Dover nearly twenty years before. As I looked back, I saw it as a reflection of strength. I had overcome many obstacles to fulfill that dream from long ago. It was a visible symbol of how those obstacles were, in fact, God-given opportunities for growth.

Terri loved the old Victorian homes in town. When I drove by one of them with a For Sale sign out front one day, I called the real estate agent and made an appointment to see it. After touring the house and the property, I knew it was perfect for her. The agent agreed to stay at the house while I went to get Terri. Although she was busy working on a system, I insisted that she come with me. And the rest was history as she purchased the house the following week.

Along with some friends that we had met while working, Terri and I had joined a local country dancing group. We both started dating, although she was much more serious about it than I was. I was not at all interested in getting involved with anyone.

I had lost my grandmothers and my aunt Mamie. The depth of my sadness honored the love I had for them, and I missed them terribly. During these years, death still frightened me. Its vast finality had no limits; it was forever. I thought the void left behind could not be filled. That space remains empty; the love, the happy times, the hugs are gone.

But there was so much I was thankful for as my faith in a loving God had grown deeper. I had difficulty finding the right words to express my gratitude when I prayed, but I was sure God knew my heart.

*****

Reflections

1. How we look at a situation determines how we will experience it. Describe a time when, if you had responded differently, a situation could have had a much different outcome.

2. Oftentimes, we enter into relationships with the hope of getting some type of benefit from them. Describe a time when you entered a relationship with only a desire to *bring* something important to it.

3. Positive energy attracts positive energy. We create this energy through our thoughts, feelings, and actions. What steps have you taken to develop an attitude of gratitude, hopefulness, and courage?

CHAPTER 8

Hello, Goodbye

Terri and I continued to be very busy with our business. Most of our work consisted of providing ongoing system support for clients we had supported for several years. Since generic systems were now flooding the market and our number of new clients had declined, we decided to inform all clients of our intent to close our business in ninety days.

After this announcement, it was such a relief to have our workload begin to diminish. We realized that we actually yearned for a calmer life. We needed to disengage from the constant productivity and give our souls a rest. We continued country dancing with friends whenever we had the time. Terri was getting quite serious about a guy she had met several months before.

When I arrived home from dancing one evening, there was a message on my voicemail. A man's voice said, "If you ever want to go parking at McGee Run, give me a call." Then he left a phone number that I didn't recognize. I thought it must be a wrong number, so I just ignored it.

About 2:00 a.m., I sat straight up in bed and said out loud, "McGee Run?" That was a favorite parking place for Tom and me during high school! I got up and listened to the message again. I tossed and turned for hours and was glad to see daylight. Then I listened intently to the message several more times, but I couldn't be sure if it was Tom's voice. Out of courtesy, I decided to call and let the man know he had the wrong number.

It was not a wrong number. It was Tom! He had been to visit my sister Kathy and her family, and he had asked about me. She told him I was divorced, and that he should give me a call sometime. As we talked, I was sure we were jumping all over the place because there was so much that had happened! He didn't mention the war, which I thought was strange; instead, he just asked me a lot of questions. How was I? Was my business doing well? How old were the kids? Had I done any traveling? What did I do in my spare time? His voice was somewhat timid, and he said he didn't want to take up a lot of my time. It was difficult to control my thoughts as the years came racing back. Then he asked if he could call again.

He called the next day. Our conversation lasted three hours as we talked about the past twenty-five years. This time, he was more relaxed, and he talked about the war. Since I had plans to visit my parents in Northwestern Pennsylvania in a couple of weeks, he asked if he could stop by and see me there. After I said yes, I didn't think about much else for the next two weeks!

Over the years, I had told Terri about Tom, so I was anxious to tell her about the conversation with him. She was shocked. When she jokingly suggested that Tom and I might get back together, we both laughed.

During the next two weeks, I felt a range of emotions. I mentally relived the past years over and over. I was nervous and apprehensive one minute and excited the next. During our last phone conversation, Tom had talked a little about the horrors he had experienced during the Vietnam War. I instantly felt guilty about being in Florida and Hawaii and so removed from the war. I certainly had thought about him over the years. But once I had become so wrapped up in my own life, I often felt quite distant from it all. I wondered how I might tell him that.

Tom called again to confirm the date I was traveling to my parents' home. The day after I arrived, I was sitting on the porch swing with Mom when he drove up in front of the house. I watched him get out of his truck, and my heart started racing. I felt my blood pressure go up, and my knees got weak! It was as if time had stood still. I was not prepared for such a reaction. I was startled when Mom said, "Well, go meet him!"

We hugged. Then we hugged again. He walked up on the porch and hugged Mom. She was happy to see him, but she wasn't as happy as I was! We saw each other every day over the next week. We took long rides through the countryside where we had enjoyed so many good times. We packed a picnic lunch and ate by the creek where we used to wash his car. We took long canoe rides down the river and enjoyed the peacefulness that we had both loved so much while growing up.

When it was time to go home, Tom asked me if he could come to Dover for a visit. Of course I said yes! As soon as I got back home, the first thing I wanted to do was to tell Terri. When she saw me, she knew instantly what had happened. She was so excited and said she couldn't wait to meet him. When I told her that would happen soon, she laughed.

Over the next several months, every weekend, either Tom came to visit me, or I went to Pittsburgh to visit him. On my first trip to see him, as I approached the Pennsylvania turnpike exit tollgates, I heard a lot of horns honking. Once I got closer to the gate, I saw Tom standing by his truck along the roadside and waving to the drivers passing by. Leaning up against him was a large sheet of plywood, and written across it in large black letters was "Welcome to Pittsburgh, Mary Lynn. I love you." I laughed right out loud, and my heart jumped for joy!

It felt quite natural to be back together again. I was thrilled when he asked me to look for an apartment for him near my home. He quit his job, loaded his truck with a few of his belongings, and made a final trip to Dover.

We got married the next summer, and the months leading up to it were like living a fairy tale. Every day was more cherished than the day before. There were days when I had to pinch myself to believe what was happening. He was just as attentive and openly affectionate as he had been all those years ago, and I loved every minute of it.

Tom moved into an apartment about fifteen miles away and began to look for work. Although my days were filled with normal daily routines, it was the evenings and weekends that we both longed for as we tried to believe the unbelievable. Had it really been twenty-five years since we had been together? There was no need to get reacquainted. The love, the humor, the feeling of being completely comfortable and secure had all returned in an instant. We enjoyed long rides and walks, yard work, fixing dinner; every mundane activity felt special. He built a deck on the back of my home, and we spent hours sitting on it and talking. We talked a lot about God and how our faith, even under the worst of circumstances, had kept an underlying hope alive, although we had not been fully aware of it. We were in awe as we talked about the choices we had made over the years, only to find our way back to each other.

We had a party at my home the night before our wedding. Everyone in both of our families attended. Since we all knew one another, it was a joyous reunion with nearly one hundred family members and friends attending. The conversations were lively as we all recalled fond memories of growing up. I didn't know it, but many of our family members had seen one another over the years at various high school reunions.

We got married in the Presbyterian church that I had attended with the kids over the years. The weather was warm and sunny, and the day was filled with laughter, hugs, and new memories. Also, an old memory popped up at our reception when Tom and I danced to "Unchained Melody." It felt as though another circle in life had just been completed.

Terri and I hugged and laughed just as we had done so often over the years. Initially, she had been concerned about my getting married so quickly after so much time had passed. But now, she said she knew it was the right thing after all. When I heard that from Terri, who had seen me through some of the worst times of my life, it meant more to me than I could explain.

As the weeks passed by, Tom and I continued to feel God's presence in our lives. We often talked about "the master plan" and how God must have always intended for us to be together. We were not teenagers any longer, and there was a profound depth to our love. We were both overwhelmed with gratitude, and our thankfulness deepened each and every day.

Our lives had been so different. I could not comprehend the horror and fear that Tom had experienced in Vietnam. He started crying as he told me about being on Hill 55, which was located near the town of Da Nang. His construction unit had been attached to a division of marines. "Hanoi Hannah" was a Vietnamese radio personality during the war, known for broadcasting English-speaking propaganda to the American troops. Tom was in camp one night when her voice came over the radio and said, "Tom Miller, you are going to die tomorrow."

Although this was a fairly common scare tactic at the time, Tom said he was not aware of it. He was nineteen years old and extremely frightened when he heard her say his name. "Tom Miller" is a fairly common American name, so she no doubt struck terror in the hearts of more than one young man that evening.

The appalling rejection that he felt when he had returned home from the war was almost as shocking as the events Tom had experienced during the war. Unlike the hero status given to returning veterans from World War II, those who served in Vietnam were portrayed as baby killers and warmongers. There were no heroes' welcome home for them. Vietnam had been a very unpopular war; however, the men and women who fought that war were only following orders. The politicians who had sent them there and then lied to the public for years should have been the ones treated with such hatred and contempt. The consequences of their lies have impacted the lives of families for generations.

Tom had been lost for years, years filled with alcohol, nightmares of war, anger, hatred, and low self-esteem. These were all symptoms of post-traumatic stress disorder (PTSD). Since the war, he had traveled the country moving from one job to another. Eventually, he had settled in Pittsburgh and gone to work for a large construction company. He lived in one of the company warehouses.

My heart broke every time he talked about those years. By the time we were married, he had not had a drink in eleven years. But he had not overcome his PTSD. For the first year of our marriage, I heard about the war every single day, multiple times a day. He was truly still suffering. Eventually, he joined a local veterans' PTSD support group that met weekly. He looked forward to talking with other guys who had experienced similar trauma, and there were so many of them.

We completed massive amounts of bureaucratic paperwork required to get him help through the Veterans Administration (VA). Tom was eligible for a primary-care doctor, certain prescriptions, and psychological counseling. But he needed additional help, and the bureaucracy within the VA was staggering.

As I helped him complete the endless government forms, I learned about his numerous episodes of pneumonia, his nightmares about the war, his feelings of quilt for being frightened. Every event had to be thoroughly documented. I reacted to his feelings; when he became angry, I was angry. When he cried, I cried.

His applications were lost or misfiled numerous times, and we had to resubmit the same paperwork repeatedly. We even drove to the navy archives in Washington, DC, to do some research on his time of service. He actually had to prove he had been in Vietnam!

After applications were processed, they were denied, and we relentlessly filed appeals. There was one stall tactic after another for months. It felt like the government just wanted these veterans to die. I was thoroughly disgusted with the bureaucracy and urged Tom to quit putting himself through the continued rejection, now from his own government, but he never gave up.

While looking for permanent employment, he worked on a few construction jobs around Dover, but none of them had any opportunity for advancement. He had learned carpentry in the navy, and he loved it. He always smiled and said, "Jesus was a carpenter."

Tom eventually decided to open his own home remodeling business. Since Terri and I had closed our business, I had accepted a position at the state's technology department, and she had accepted a job with the state police credit union.

The year after Tom and I were married, Terri married the man she had met during our country-dancing days. Roy was nearly twenty-five years older than her. I thought their age difference might cause problems in the years ahead, but she was in love, and she assured me their marriage would be fine. I had my doubts, particularly when they sold her Victorian home that she loved so much and moved into a large modern home in the next town.

Tom was finally admitted into a veteran-sponsored PTSD detox facility near Chesapeake Bay in Maryland. He was an inpatient for three months of intense psychological therapy. He thought the most helpful part of the therapy was the "sweat lodge," a tepee-shaped canvas structure that was heated by hot rocks placed in the center of it. The patients sat in a circle on the ground around the rocks. Based upon a purification ritual used by Native American Indians, the intent was to eliminate or reduce deep anxiety through intense prayer and healing sessions. Tom also needed to release the guilt he felt for being frightened during the war. He was a nineteen-year-old kid when he was thrown into a war in the middle of a jungle. Who wouldn't be afraid?

After he completed the PTSD-detox program, Tom was much more at peace, but he still had *triggers* that he tried to overcome. The sound of a helicopter overhead made him very anxious. When he felt someone following too closely behind us while out shopping, we had to stop and let them pass by. But he was still much more at ease now, and he no longer talked about the war every day. Our lives settled into a peaceful routine. There was a calmness and order to everyday life.

When we were in high school, Tom had been so openly affectionate. Our friends used to tease me about how he always made such a fuss over me. It was plain to see that he hadn't changed at all where that was concerned. I never knew when or where he was going to unexpectedly say something affectionate. While checking out at the grocery store one day, he handed the cashier money, and then he turned around and pointed to me. "Do you know how much I love this lady?" he asked the cashier.

Of course, the cashier smiled as she looked at me. Just like those years so long ago, it was still rather embarrassing at times…but I loved it!

Tom's business was doing well, as was my new job. Terri and Roy and Tom and I continued with our evenings of dancing for only a few weeks. Alcohol was served at the dance hall, and it was unfair to subject Tom to that kind of environment. He was willing to go, but I knew it made him uncomfortable, so our dancing days faded away. Although I missed the fun, I mostly missed the kiss on my forehead that he would give after each slow dance.

Terri and Roy were busy making a new life, but we still had good times together, and Tom's famous belly laugh was back. We all had fun just laughing at him laughing!

Our peaceful life was punctured when Dad called one day to let me know that Mom had recently had some unexpected falls. When he took her to the doctor, she was diagnosed with Parkinson's disease. This was a tremendous blow to our entire family. It was the first serious illness of any kind for us, and it was especially upsetting because it was Mom. Mom—the one who had packed lunches for eight kids; the one who had ironed clothes, fixed meals, and nursed all of us through measles, mumps, and chicken pox; the one who had never missed sending a birthday card; the one who had counted the days until she could hug her grandkids.

All eight of us "kids" were now grown with families of our own, but we had all returned home for frequent visits. We were a close-knit family, and our parents were the glue that held us together.

After Mom's diagnosis, our joyous visits were dampened by a sense of foreboding. Her health declined slowly and steadily. Initially, she used a cane for walking. She hated that cane because she was so used to an active and busy life. Many times, she defiantly refused to use it. Still, her wonderful sense of humor and positive attitude were intact. I was in awe at how she handled the disease.

Eventually, Mom needed a walker to get around. She hated the walker even more than the cane. She knew she needed to use it, but her memory was failing. Sometimes she simply forgot about it and started walking. Frustration and worry filled Dad's days. The disease was obviously taking its toll on him as well.

The trips back to Dover were solemn as I tried to imagine a life without Mom. Tom's mother had suffered a stroke after his discharge from the navy, and he had spent years taking care of her. He knew only too well about the emotional roller coaster of a serious illness. He was a great comfort to me. Once back home, I was grateful for our busy lives.

Tom's reputation grew by word of mouth. He had a steady stream of remodeling jobs for homes, and he was also contracted as the finishing carpenter for several homes being built in new housing developments in the area. He worked weekends just to stay on schedule. My job became more demanding as I was assigned to troubled projects and expected to get them back on track. Terri's job was less demanding, and since Roy was retired, she spent more time at home. We didn't see each other very often, but we always made it a point to call every few days.

Mom's health continued to decline, and she was soon confined to a wheelchair. The dementia worsened. During my visits, I walked out of the house many times to be alone. My heart ached. I could not control the tears as I watched her slowly slip away.

During one of our visits, I asked Mom if she would give me some good advice that I should always remember. She was in her wheelchair; she looked right at me, smiled, and said, "Always be positive. Always be faithful. Never give up."

Always be positive. Even with the daily stress of raising such a large family, Mom was always positive. She never said a harsh word and was somehow able to find the best in each day.

Always be faithful. Mom and Dad had been married for over fifty years. They still held hands while watching TV. She was devoted to him.

Never give up. Mom was fiercely fighting this disease, and I didn't think she was ready to die. I know her mind was slowly slipping away, so how could I really know? Still, she was lucid enough to give such thoughtful advice. It was a moment I will never forget, and it is advice that I have passed on to others over the years.

Regardless of the weather, Mom loved to sit on the front porch swing. We were swinging one day when she asked me if I saw the little girl walking down the sidewalk all by herself. Mom was worried that no one was with her. I looked, and there was no little girl.

I didn't tell Mom that; instead, I assured her she was okay. Mom frequently spoke of this little girl and worried about her being alone. My older brother had a twin sister who had died when she was only two days old. I often wondered if the little girl that Mom saw was, in fact, the little baby she had lost so long ago.

I was struck by this awareness. Was Mom's mind taking her back to those years long ago, or was her soul letting her remember the love that she had felt for her baby girl? Awareness is such a vital aspect of living, and oftentimes, we miss valuable messages. The disease was obviously progressing with these hallucinations. Although it was sad to see Mom slowly slip away, it was comforting to think she may have had some peaceful memories.

As she approached her eightieth birthday, I had a most poignant experience with her. We had been talking one evening when I remembered the very first time—and the only time—that I had ever lied to her.

Although I was only ten years old, I felt protective of my little sister Betty Ann. She was four years younger than me, small and skinny for her age, and unusually shy. It was a warm, sunny early fall day with flowers still in full bloom all over the countryside. On this particular day, Betty Ann came home in tears from playing with Paula, a loud and bossy neighborhood girl. I didn't know what Paula said or did to hurt her feelings, but it didn't matter because I was determined to do something about it. But what could I do to get even with her?

Paula lived on the other side of the old baseball field about half a mile down the road. Her mother, also loud and bossy, was very proud of the flower garden she had created in their backyard. Suddenly, it felt like the perfect target for some misguided revenge! So on that fateful day, I crept down alongside the old overgrown ball field because I thought no one would see me. Hoping Paula would get in trouble for playing out there, I furiously destroyed a large part of the flower garden. I then ran home as fast as I could, feeling quite satisfied that this was the perfect solution for avenging my sister's tears.

Much to my surprise, Paula's mother soon stormed down to our house, came angrily through the back door and into our kitchen, and in that piercing, annoying voice, she told my mother what I had done. I was caught off guard with no time to think of any believable explanation, but I was positive no one had seen me. When Mom turned and calmly asked me if I had done such a terrible thing, I lied. I said I knew nothing about it.

I didn't lie because I was afraid of getting into trouble; that wasn't it at all. As Mom stood in front of me, I looked into her vivid blue eyes, so full of love and goodness, and I only lied because I didn't want her to be disappointed in me. In that instant, I saw the stark difference between my mother and Paula's mother, and for the first time, I felt sorry for Paula.

Mom obviously believed me, and she politely told Paula's mother that she must be mistaken. She complimented her on her garden and said she was sorry someone had done such a senseless act. I felt so relieved as Paula's mother indignantly spun around on her heel and stomped out of the kitchen. I never forgot that day or how deeply loved I felt. And I never lied to my mother again.

Now, after all these years, I finally recounted this lie to her. We were alone, and she was in her wheelchair. Her eyes weren't quite as bright as they had been on that day long ago, but she looked right at me, and her smile was just as sweet. She didn't say a word, but I knew then that she had known my little secret for over forty years!

Ultimately, Mom became bedridden. During those visits, she didn't recognize me. I sat and talked to her for hours, but she didn't talk back. The only thing that remained of Mom was her endearing smile.

The dreaded phone call came in early September. Tom and I immediately headed for my parents' home. Betty Ann, who was a nurse, had been staying with them, and she called to let us all know that Mom was dying. Most of my siblings were able to make it home in time. Along with Dad, we surrounded Mom's bed. I had my hand on her leg, and I watched her take her last breath.

I had prayed this wouldn't happen so soon. It didn't feel like she had been sick for seven years. It felt like just yesterday that she had been healthy and active and running a busy household. So many childhood memories came rushing back.

After a short time, I walked out on the back porch and sobbed. I had been so fearful of this moment. No amount of preparation could have lessened the pain I felt. Mom was gone.

I had a favorite place where I often went to pray when we visited Mom and Dad, and I walked there the next day. The road was two blocks from our house, and the first mile was uphill. At the top of the hill, the road leveled off with thick, tall pine trees lining both sides. I had constantly felt closer to God on top of that hill. Standing among the tall trees, I had always felt a soft breeze. It was warm in the summer and cold in the winter, but it was always there. It sounded like the trees were whispering to one another.

I stood there for what seemed like the longest time, and there was no breeze, only silence. But then that gentle breeze began to blow. I closed my eyes and felt its gentleness on my face. I pretended I was one of the trees, and that soft whispering breeze quietly and effortlessly touched my soul. I prayed a prayer of thankfulness for the mother who had loved me so deeply.

The next few days were filled with funeral arrangements, friends and family stopping by with food, and flowers arriving at the front door. I was in a daze and felt as though all the strength had been drained from my body.

I had a five-year-old nephew, Rossie, who cherished his grandmother. How was he going to understand that she was gone? We sat together on a velvet-cushioned bench at the funeral home, both of us crying, and then I asked him if he wanted to go for a walk. We started up the street hand in hand, and I told him a story I had once heard. It was about a little boy standing next to Jesus, and they were watching a long line of people climbing up the mountainside. They were all ages, and most of them had a bag thrown over their shoulder. Some of the bags were light and flimsy, and the people scurried up the mountain. Other bags appeared to be quite full, and those people were moving more slowly and struggling. Still others were stooped over under the burden of extremely heavy bags. They had to stop and rest every few steps. Their faces looked fearful and worried, as if they weren't sure they could make it to the top. "Where is everyone going?" the little boy asked.

Jesus smiled and replied, "They are on their way to heaven."

The little boy looked confused and asked, "But why do some of them have such heavy bags to carry?"

Jesus put the little boy on his lap and said, "Those bags have tears in them. The people carrying the heavy bags are the ones who left behind very sad people who miss them and cry for them all the time."

Rossie pushed his glasses up on his forehead and wiped his eyes. He looked up at me and said, "We don't want Grandma to carry a heavy bag, do we?"

I picked him up, hugged him, and said, "No, Rossie, we don't. We want Grandma to be happy as she travels to heaven. She will be with us every time we think of her."

As we walked back to the funeral home hand in hand, I knew I had told that story as much for me as for Rossie.

One week after Mom died, the 9/11 terrorist attacks occurred in New York; Washington, DC; and Pennsylvania. I was grateful that Mom, who always found the best in everyone and everything, hadn't had to witness such horror.

Once we were home in Dover, life resumed with the normal daily activities and commitments. Somehow, that didn't seem right. My mind and my heart could not reconcile the fact that Mom was gone. How could routine office meetings continue as usual when I had just lost such an important part of my life? When I walked around our neighborhood, I heard kids playing and dogs barking just as they had always done, but things were different now. Even though my world had changed, life around me continued on as if nothing had happened. The world kept spinning. It wasn't right.

Since I was the second eldest of eight children, I considered myself to be luckier than most of my siblings simply because I had gotten to spend more years with Mom. I got to feel more of her warm hugs and see more of her sweet smiles. I watched her manage a busy household with daily demands that kept her busy from early morning until late at night.

As a teenager, I often grumbled about my having to do "just about everything" around the house. I remembered the old wicker laundry basket that used to set near the ironing board in a small back room in our home. I don't think the ironing board was ever put away. I remember Mom saying that she hadn't seen the bottom of that basket for over thirty years! It wasn't until I had children of my own that I finally realized how her selfless sacrifices had such an influence on who I had become.

I worried about Dad. The past seven years had been challenging for him in so many ways. Except for his time away during World War II, they had never been apart. We continued to make frequent trips back to visit him. I had never seen my dad cry before, and our conversations at the kitchen table were gut-wrenching. I tried to imagine what it felt like to lose your spouse. It was inconceivable to me.

As I longed for that part of my life that was gone, new lives started. Andy and Michelle had graduated from college. They had both married, and their families and jobs kept them busy. I was so proud of both of them. And Tom loved them as if they were his own children.

He and I routinely talked about how they had each grown into such responsible adults. We also talked about parenting and how puzzling it can be as you try to learn and to accept who they really are becoming. It's remarkable how different two siblings can be, or maybe it's just the difference between boys and girls. But I always laughed when I thought about how each of them got engaged. After days of hiking, Andy proposed to Kasey on the floor of the Grand Canyon! He had packed her engagement ring and a bottle of champagne in his backpack in preparation for the special event. Michelle always loved the city, perhaps because we had made several annual Christmas trips to New York City when she was young. So when Mike proposed to her, they were at the top of the Empire State Building!

We both marveled at watching them grow. Tom's kind and loving personality was a good influence on them as young adults. I thought about how they had visited their grandmother during the summer months as small children. I knew Mom was smiling and still watching over them from heaven.

A few days after Mom died, Tom called from the local emergency room. Sudden chest pains had caused him to leave his jobsite and drive to the local hospital. I immediately joined him there, where we spent hours while he underwent a series of tests. The cardiologist finally confirmed that he had had a heart attack, and the damage to his heart was irreparable. I felt numb.

*****

Hovering over these years brought back the feeling of one of the highest points in my life, which was when Tom reappeared after twenty-five years. And it brought back a feeling of one of the lowest points in my life, which was when Mom died. And then it brought back the feeling of immense apprehension of what might be next for us after Tom's heart attack. What I remembered most about these years was praying to a loving God.

I prayed often with a most grateful heart for the blessings in my life. I was so thankful for two children, grown into responsible young adults with families of their own. I thought about how Mom loved little kids, and I often told our grandkids how happy their great-grandmother was as she looked down from heaven and smiled at them.

I thanked God for Terri. I had been completely happy being a single mother, owning my own business, and having Terri and the kind of friendship most people never experience. I had heard many times that friends should never go into business together because the stress can ruin the relationship; however, it was *because* Terri and I were such close friends that our business thrived.

I thanked God for Mom. She had lived her life with a positive attitude, a measure of kindness that endeared her to everyone who knew her, and a sense of humor that kept us laughing for years. She had been such an important and influential role model. She had a deep faith in God. She never complained about her busy life raising eight children. Her energy and love for life were undeniable. Her spirit lives within me still.

I thanked God for bringing Tom back into my life. I had thought that I couldn't be any happier…until Tom reappeared. Because we had known each other in high school and were once engaged, our reunion was much more meaningful. We had both been married and divorced, so we had a deeper appreciation for the challenges that life brings. He had suffered the effects of the war for so many years; that awareness alone gave me a deeper sense of gratitude for my own life.

I had grown quite accustomed to the calm and happy life that Tom and I had made together. His sudden heart attack had disrupted that peacefulness. The uncertainty of our future became my new reality.

*****

Reflections

1. A serious health problem can disrupt all aspects of our lives. Have you ever had to deal with the range of emotions related to the apprehension of what was now ahead? How were you able to work through it?

   _____
   _____
   _____
   _____

2. As we get older, we are often faced with more deaths of friends and family. Do you think this helps prepare us for our own death? Please explain.

   _____
   _____
   _____
   _____

3. Gratitude can be a bold approach to life. Finding something positive each day can be challenging or, at times, feel impossible. As you reflect on what has happened to you today, what can you be grateful for?

   _____
   _____
   _____
   _____

CHAPTER 9

Now What?

During Tom's two tours in Vietnam, he had been exposed to the chemical Agent Orange, which had been proven to be a contributing factor to heart disease, as well as many other diseases. Tom was in the early stages of chronic obstructive pulmonary disease (COPD). This was attributed to smoking (he had quit six years before) and exposure to asbestos and other respiratory irritants during his years in construction. The heart attack, coupled with the COPD, made it impossible for him to continue working. Now what do we do?

Life changed in an instant, and we were devastated. Tom arranged for another contractor to complete his outstanding jobs, and he sold his equipment. He had always taken such good care of his tools and equipment, and it was demoralizing for him to sell them. I told him to wait before making such a final decision; maybe he could still use some of them around the house. But he was angry at his sudden disability. With deep sadness, I watched while he sold everything.

His breathing had been seriously affected, and he was soon on oxygen twenty-four hours a day. The daytime hours bothered him the most. He had a large portable tank of oxygen with him at all times. This meant that even the simplest household chores were cumbersome. Tom was frightened and irritable. He had lost his sense of self-worth…again.

I continued to work, but my days were overshadowed with worry. Follow-up appointments with the cardiologist and the pulmonologist were not encouraging. Tom and I had long conversations about the adjustments we needed to make. He no longer had an income, and he was too young to receive social security benefits. It troubled him that he would not be contributing financially to our marriage.

For him to feel useful, we created a workable budget, and I saw some of his anxiety subside. We decided on specific small home-improvement projects that he could work on without struggling to meet any deadlines. Over time, he began to better adjust and accept his limitations.

We started the tedious process of filing disability applications with the Veterans Administration. Based upon our previous experiences, I mentally prepared myself for the frustration I knew was ahead in dealing with the government. After several months, Tom contacted the Widener University Law School, which was located forty miles away. He had learned that the law students researched military service to help veterans file claims. One of the professors reviewed Tom's case, and he agreed to accept it. He helped Tom complete the endless paperwork and advised him of the *proper* words to use on the applications. Here was the hand of God once again, that invisible, intangible presence guiding us along a path that appeared to be insurmountable.

Our life settled into a new routine, but it was a routine we never expected to face. Terri and Roy were very supportive, and we often had dinners together. The kids came to visit us frequently, and our church family offered to help in any way. Tom's sisters, both of whom he loved dearly, came to visit a few times. They reminisced about growing up, and their laughter helped his overall mood. Their visits were instrumental in encouraging him to remain optimistic. We were extremely grateful for the love shown to us by so many people.

Tom's breathing became more difficult with each passing year, but he learned to maneuver quite well around the house with the oxygen tank, fifty feet of tubing, and a nasal cannula. He completed several home projects, and I was in awe of the positive attitude he had developed.

We continued to make frequent trips to see Dad. He and Tom enjoyed doing woodworking projects together. Tom stayed with him for a couple of weeks, and with help from my brothers, he constructed a downstairs bathroom, all the while dragging an oxygen tank around.

We flew to Oregon one year to visit Andy and his family. It was a challenge to schedule a flight for someone who was on oxygen. Tom could keep his own oxygen tank but only until we arrived at the airline check-in counter. There, the clerk took his tank and gave him a new one from the airlines—for an additional cost, of course. If we had to change planes during the long flight, the airline clerk retrieved their tank upon arrival at that next airport. That meant we had to arrange for someone from the VA to meet us with a new tank. Then the same procedure was followed for the next flight! Every time we changed planes, the same process was followed. It was both unnerving and annoying.

Andy and Kasey had purchased a fixer-upper for their first home. Once Tom saw he could be useful, he wanted to help them finish the basement. I came back home because of my job, but he stayed with them for a month. He coordinated his visit with the veteran's group that was supplying his oxygen, so his tanks were delivered to Andy's house each week. The work he completed at the house was very gratifying for Tom and contributed to a greater sense of self-worth.

I flew back to Oregon to be with him on the trip home. The return flight required the same amount of coordination for his oxygen. He had adapted well to such inconveniences. I, on the other hand, prayed often for patience.

Even with increased medications, Tom's breathing worsened, and he soon needed multiple oxygen tanks whenever we went away for a few hours. He bought an old baby carriage at a yard sale one day and converted it into a two-tank cart. He took it everywhere we went. I thought this was an ingenious idea, and again, I marveled at how he had learned to accept his health limitations.

During one of his follow-up appointments, his pulmonologist suggested that we begin to look into a lung transplant program. We located one at Temple University Hospital in Philadelphia. The process to determine if he was a good candidate for a double lung transplant was extensive, requiring nearly four months of medical and psychological tests.

During the evaluation, the doctors explained that although good lungs could allow Tom to breathe freely again, other side effects or diseases might result from the powerful drugs he would be required to take after the surgery. That all sounded quite ominous at the time, but since he needed healthier lungs to live, a transplant was the only option.

Temple Hospital was located in Northern Philadelphia, so we had to drive through the city to get there. The drive could take a few hours, depending upon traffic. With the travel time and multiple doctor appointments, the average day's trip lasted about twelve hours.

All the trips, tests, and preparation were overwhelming, and Tom, of course, experienced the worst of it. I pushed him in a wheelchair for countless trips up and down the long crowded hospital hallways. They were lined with pictures and paintings of past doctors. I often felt as though they watched us as we went from one test to another, with Tom struggling to breathe and holding on to his oxygen tank. It had been almost forty years since the first lung transplant had been performed. In those early years, patients rarely survived more than a few days or weeks. Surely, technology had improved immensely since then; however, the intricate surgery was still fraught with risk.

During those long months, I was immersed in learning the complexities of the human body and the possible side effects of various medications. *Rejection* was a word that I read about and that I feared the most. Rejection is a normal reaction of the body. When a new organ is transplanted, the body's immune system treats it as a threat and produces antibodies against it. The risk of infection is higher than average because the immunosuppressant drugs weaken the immune system. Kidney disease is a common long-term complication. Diabetes, high blood pressure, and osteoporosis were also only a few of the diseases that occur more frequently in transplant patients.

Although this new knowledge was mind-boggling, I constantly prayed Tom would be eligible for the transplant. I was more afraid of losing him than I was of managing any number of potential complications.

The doctors told us that when a lung becomes available, the patient is expected to be at the hospital within two or three hours. We learned that the Delaware State Police offered free helicopter trips for transplant patients, so after Tom was placed on the regional transplant list, I registered with them. They assured me they would be available if and when we got the call.

If we got the call? During all of these months, I had never considered that he would not get called. That thought instantly increased my level of anxiety. We were both on high alert as we waited for that phone call. How long would we have to wait? How long *could* he wait? If Tom had many more lung infections that worsened his condition, he would no longer be eligible for the surgery.

The biggest concern Tom had was that he was waiting for someone to die so that he could live. I knew it haunted him. About a month after his name was placed on the transplant list, I received an early-morning call at my office from one of the nurses on the transplant team. I recognized her voice immediately, and my heart stood still. Without hesitation, she said, "We have a lung."

*****

Hovering over this time in our lives brought back a multitude of raw emotions. The news of Tom's heart attack had struck fear deep into my soul. How could this happen after all the years we had been apart? I refused to believe the seriousness of it, and I tried to convince both of us that things would get better.

It broke my heart to see him sell all of his equipment. Overnight, he had lost his career. He knew he could no longer contribute financially to our marriage. He felt alone and isolated. It was a daily struggle to try and convince him that things would be okay. And how could this happen only a week after Mom had died?

We cried, and we prayed. Tom eventually learned to accept his condition, and we created a "new normal." His lifestyle changed from a busy schedule of remodeling homes to one filled with small home projects, woodworking hobbies, and doctor appointments.

This time also brought back feelings of the intense and exhausting apprehension of waiting for him to get new lungs. Emotions ranged from hope, elation, and gratitude to fear, sadness, and helplessness. The waiting was grueling.

Someone had to die for Tom to live. We talked a lot about his feelings of guilt, and the conversation always led to wondering if he would actually live long enough to get new lungs. The reality of the situation was punishing.

I had been instructed to keep a bag packed at all times so that we could leave immediately after getting the phone call. It was an eerie feeling to see the suitcase by the back door each morning as I left for work.

I continuously thanked God for the lung transplant program that was, hopefully, going to give Tom not only a chance to live a longer and healthier life but also to give us more happy years together to watch our grandchildren grow up.

*****

Reflections

1. Have you ever had a tragic event disrupt your life? How did you respond, and what did you learn from it?

   _____
   _____
   _____
   _____

2. Worrying is a natural feeling of being overly concerned about a situation or problem. Do you try to get your worrying under control by disengaging your mind from your feelings? What strategy do you use to ease your worry? Write them down? Pray?

   _____
   _____
   _____
   _____

3. Patience allows us to manage our emotions, to persevere, and to make better decisions. Do you enjoy the benefit of patience, or do you need to work on improving that skill?

   _____
   _____
   _____
   _____

CHAPTER 10

Transplant and Transform

As soon as the phone call came from the transplant nurse that a lung was available, I called the Delaware State Police Communication Center. The officer said to come right away, and someone would meet us outside. As I drove into the parking lot, we watched a helicopter approach from the distance. The closer it got, the more nervous I felt. Once on board, there was barely enough room for the two of us, Tom's oxygen tank, and the small suitcase that had been at the back door in preparation for this moment.

The copilot helped strap us in and assured us that it would be a smooth flight. As we lifted off, he gave me a set of headphones so they could explain what was happening. I had never flown in a helicopter before, and the excitement of the moment was gripping. The noise drowned out any attempt to talk to Tom, but I knew the flight reminded him of the Vietnam War. We looked at each other and smiled.

We arrived in Philadelphia within minutes of leaving Dover. The pilot circled the hospital a couple of times, and I saw nurses below, waiting with a stretcher near the landing location on the roof of the building. I was dumbstruck as I watched this extraordinary event unfold before me.

We landed, and Tom was put on the stretcher and rolled in through the wide hospital doors. He was immediately taken to the operating room and prepped for surgery. And I waited. I was used to waiting.

After Tom's heart attack, multiple lung infections, the transplant evaluation process, dozens of trips to the hospital, and so many prayers, it now felt as though there might be an end in sight. The nurse's words, "We have a lung," echoed through my mind.

During the evaluation process, the transplant doctors had been very specific in explaining that occasionally, a donated lung will not be an exact match for the patient. This could be for any number of reasons, including blood type, organ and chest cavity size, tissue type, and medical condition of the patient. Time is of the essence, and the patient must stand by as doctors make that final determination for crossmatch compatibility. I knew Tom was undergoing that process right now, and my heart raced.

After a few hours, I was notified that the lungs were not a good match for Tom. My heart sank. Was all of this anticipation and worry for nothing? How could that be? The doctor reminded me how this sometimes happens, but his words rang hollow in the stillness of the waiting room.

I sat by the window and looked out over the city, the traffic lights turning from red to yellow to green over and over again. Traffic stopped and then moved forward. I saw a garbage truck on the street below and watched men empty large trash cans into the back of it. Occasionally, a fire truck or an ambulance went screaming by. It was just another normal night for the city, but it wasn't for us.

The nurse took me to a room on the pulmonary ward, and I waited. After a few more hours, Tom came through in a wheelchair pushed by a nurse. After the nurse left, we sat in silence in the early-morning hours.

Terri was sick, so we called Michelle to come and take us home. On the ride back, I knew what Tom was thinking. *Who did those lungs belong to? What happened to make them available?*

When we got home, I put the small suitcase back by the back door and wondered when we would need it again. But it had been such a physically and emotionally draining day that I was too tired to think about it for very long. We both just wanted the day to end.

A few days later, Tom contracted a serious lung infection and was hospitalized at Temple again. I drove back and forth every day for over a week to be with him. When he improved enough to come home, he was given a life expectancy of only a few weeks. His name was moved further up on the transplant list.

Two weeks later, the transplant nurse called again. For the second time, I heard, "We have a lung." It was late in the day, and I was still at my office. I called Tom and told him to get ready, and then I called the state police again. I drove home, grabbed that suitcase by the door, and we were on our way.

It was a larger helicopter this time—a little more room, a little less noise, a little more time to look at each other and hope. It was also a different helicopter crew, but again, they were so comforting and caring. How do you properly thank strangers at such a time as this?

We landed on the hospital roof once again as the nurses waited with a stretcher. We hugged and said, "See you later," and Tom was whisked off to the operating room.

The hours limped by as I aimlessly wandered through the hospital halls. I walked outside into the humid August night and silently prayed. I walked back in and unconsciously leafed through magazines. I had several cups of coffee. I looked up at the large round clock on the waiting room wall. It was 2:00 a.m.

Five hours later, the surgeon came in and told me that everything went well, and Tom was in intensive care. When I was finally able to see him, I was shocked at how terrible he looked. He was still under the anesthesia, so there was no movement or eye contact. He looked so frail with hoses in his arms, nose, and chest. The large cold room was dimly lit and full of blinking and beeping equipment. The nurses were busy checking hoses and various medical equipment. It suddenly felt as though I had been watching a movie, the one where a sick patient is being whisked off to a hospital in a helicopter; nurses are waiting to take him to surgery; a clock is ticking on the waiting room wall; hospital staff are coming in and out for shift changes; a patient is being brought back to a room and hooked up to various machines—and the family is praying.

The doctor explained that Tom had received only one lung. The donor had requested that two patients each receive one lung. Although Tom needed two lungs, the doctor said he was too sick and could not afford to wait any longer, so they replaced the lung that was in the worse condition.

My daily trips from home to the hospital continued. In less than two weeks, Tom walked out the front door of the hospital—this time, with no oxygen tanks! He was ecstatic. Once we were home, he stayed up all night, walking around the house, breathing freely. He couldn't sit still. He went up and down the stairs with a big smile on his face. I felt like I was in a trance as he paraded by me time and time again. We hugged and kissed without that oxygen hose in his nose. We found an *oldies* channel on the radio, and we blissfully danced to "Unchained Melody." The profound disappointment just two weeks before had been replaced with sheer joy and unfathomable gratitude. I thanked God with tears rolling down my face.

Tom's medication regimen was staggering. He had two powerful drugs to prevent organ rejection. Those doses changed almost daily, depending upon his blood work. He now had drug-induced diabetes, so I gave him insulin shots twice a day. He was still on a megadose of steroids. There were drugs for blood pressure, stomach irritation, anxiety, sleep, pain, and more. When I got the first prescriptions filled, I bought a large pillbox, latex gloves, a pill splitter, and a notebook to keep track of things. Our kitchen table looked like a pharmacy.

For the first two weeks, we were supposed to go back to the hospital every day for blood work and checkups, but Tom had been home for only two days when he developed a fever, and I called 911. As soon as we arrived at the local emergency room, the doctor called the transplant nurse in Philadelphia. Local hospitals want nothing to do with transplant patients because of potential complications. Within an hour, Tom was taken via helicopter back to Temple Hospital. I drove up and spent two days with him before going back home long enough to get a few hours of rest. My daily trips back to the hospital continued for the next two weeks.

TRANSPLANT AND TRANSFORM

During the first year after the transplant, I felt as though I lived in Philadelphia because Tom was hospitalized several times. Each day, as I waited for visiting hours to open on the pulmonary ward, I went for long walks around the city. Many days, I walked down by the river that ran between Philadelphia and New Jersey.

I had found a secluded place to rest along the water. It was protected from the hot summer sun and insulated from the wind and snow during the winter months. It became my special place to talk to God. I didn't just pray while sitting there; I actually *talked* to God. I talked about how Tom had suffered so much after the war and how his suffering was now continuing after the surgery. I wondered how he had the strength to withstand being hospitalized so many times. I said how tired I was, and I hoped we could go home soon. I didn't ask God why about any of it just yet. I simply let God know that I didn't quite understand all that was happening. It helped to sit in that quiet place and talk out loud.

Tom's hospitalizations were related to various complications and side effects of the drugs. Once I lined up all his pill bottles on the table, they looked like a small army of brown plastic soldiers with white caps. It was a challenge to keep the pillbox filled with the most recent prescriptions because they were modified so frequently. I was grateful to have good health insurance because the monthly cost of some drugs was several thousand dollars.

I constantly filled the pillbox after multiple trips, sometimes daily, to the pharmacy. The nurse had shown me how to give Tom his insulin shots, but the process still made me nervous. I knew I had to get used to this new regimen, and I prayed that I could do it without making a serious mistake.

As I filled the pillbox late one evening, I realized I had misjudged one of the dosages, and there was not enough medicine for the following morning. I drove to the twenty-four-hour drugstore and explained the situation to the pharmacist. When she was unable to get approval from our insurance company, I just stood at the counter and cried. I'm sure it was an angel wearing that long white pharmacy coat that night because against all rules, she gave me just enough pills for the morning.

Since I thought I had done something wrong, I called the nurse the next morning. She explained why that often happens, particularly during the first year, and she called in a new prescription. Because the dosage had changed as a result of Tom's blood work, the prescription had merely run out early. It was another lesson learned in managing his medications.

The daily demands both at work and at home were overwhelming, and I was under a great deal of stress. I knew I would eventually make a serious mistake either at work or at home, and I didn't want to take that chance. Ten months after the transplant, I decided to retire.

Retirement was such a reflective decision. Although I knew it was necessary, I knew I would be losing a very important part of my life. I had entered the fascinating world of technology as a young keypunch operator while in the air force. The keypunch machine, the punched-card accounting machines, and the second-, third-, and fourth-generation computers and programming languages that I had worked with were now mostly obsolete. You could find some of the equipment in the Smithsonian Institute!

I had witnessed the introduction of email and the beginning of the World Wide Web. Some of the early programming languages I had coded were FORTRAN, RPG, COBOL, and Basic Assembler. More advanced languages included Perl, dBase, C++, Java, Adabas, and eventually, the launch of Google. Reading memory dumps to interpret testing results initially required an understanding of binary, octal, and hexadecimal numbering systems, but eventually, the system-testing results were printed out in plain English!

My forty-five-year career in technology spanned from those initial keypunching days, to owning my own computer software business, to managing multimillion-dollar system implementations. And my initial excitement in those early days never waned. As technology advanced in so many areas, it always felt as though I was at just the right place at just the right time. It was God's timing that had led me through those forty-five years, and now it was God's timing calling me to become the caregiver for the love of my life.

I had learned a great deal about the physical challenges Tom would face and the new diseases he might contract, but I was unprepared for the psychological effect the transplant had on him. Because he had been hospitalized several times already, he was worried that his body would eventually reject the new lung. He felt guilty because he had someone else's lung in his chest. He also felt guilty because I was burdened with so much responsibility to ensure that he stayed healthy. And he was always troubled by the unending disability denials that steadily arrived from the Veterans Administration.

I continued to research the side effects of all new drugs. I also became well aware of the signs to look for when Tom needed a trip to the doctor's office or lab or when a 911 call was necessary or simply when I needed the nurse to answer a question or reassure me. In the middle of so many nights, I silently thanked our cherished doctors, nurses, helicopter pilots, family, and friends. I thanked the young man who had died in a car accident and had donated his lung, and I thanked God for all of these people who had become such an important part of our lives.

After nearly a year of complications and hospitalizations, Tom's physical health became more stable. I thought a change of scenery might take his mind off his worries, so I suggested we take a trip across the country. We could take our time, enjoy the scenery, and visit Andy and his family in Oregon. Tom agreed wholeheartedly, and his attitude improved immediately.

After a few days of planning and with the approval of the transplant doctor, we packed the back of Tom's truck with suitcases, ice chests, food and water, lawn chairs, laptop, my thick pharmacy notebook, and bags of drugs. We had no reservations but instead decided to stop for the night whenever we felt like it. We had no idea how long we would be gone.

Terri was relieved that we had decided to get away because she knew only too well how demanding the past year had been for us. She was my "sounding board," and her positive attitude had helped me maintain a relatively calm environment at home. When Tom had a change in medication, she would promptly point out that new and better drugs were becoming available. When Tom was admitted to the hospital, she noted that he would come home feeling better. It reminded me of those chaotic days during my first marriage when she had been such a source of strength. But she had been sick again lately, and I was also worried about her health.

The first stop on our trip across the country was to visit Dad. He was thrilled to see Tom breathing normally and not hampered by the presence of an oxygen tank. Although he missed Mom terribly, Dad had kept busy with a multitude of projects in his workshop, and I was relieved to see him busy doing what he loved. A few days later and with a lighter heart, I checked all the vacation paraphernalia in the back of the truck, and we headed west.

We took the northern route out, and two weeks later, we arrived in Seattle. Along the way, we spent some time near Lake Michigan. We spent a particularly beautiful day in Wisconsin where we bought some cheese and crackers at a local shop and sat on a park bench near the Mississippi River. We actually hiked for a short time in the Badlands of South Dakota and marveled at the grandeur of Mount Rushmore. We loved spending a couple of days at a small town in Montana nestled at the edge of Glacier National Park. The trip was certainly an improvement over the grueling daily routine at home. We often expressed our gratitude for this adventure and for the opportunity to marvel at the beauty of God's creation.

Since Tom needed blood work done every week, I searched online for the location of a Labcorp facility, and we made those cities or towns one of our overnight stops. The lab results were faxed back to the nurse at Temple Hospital, and she called me if any medications needed to be adjusted. I was pleasantly surprised at the ease in handling this while traveling.

When we arrived in Seattle, Tom had a fever, so I took him to the local emergency room. Once the doctor reviewed his list of medications and realized he was a transplant patient, he called the nurse at Temple Hospital, and Tom was admitted. Over the next three days, he had pulmonary tests and more blood work done. I visited him each morning and then walked around the city, sightseeing in the afternoons. I spent hours at the Pike Place Market in the center of downtown, visited the Seattle Space Needle, and wandered through the Tropical Butterfly House at the Pacific Science Center. I went back to the hospital each evening.

It was late summer, and the weather was beautiful. As I walked around the city on a sunny afternoon, I suddenly felt as though someone was following me. But instead of feeling nervous, I felt extremely peaceful. When I realized that it was my own shadow that was following me, I strangely felt God's presence in a very visible way! I felt protected. I felt hopeful. And even until this day, I get a comforting feeling when I'm out walking with my shadow.

After Tom was discharged with some new medications, we went on to Portland and visited Andy and his family for a few days. Tom's transplant doctor instructed the Seattle doctor to make arrangements for him to get follow-up tests at a Portland hospital. While I was on the phone with nurses from all three facilities at the same time, I wondered again if I would ever get used to this new lifestyle.

The trip back to Dover was uneventful, except for a change in medication that I had to get filled at a pharmacy in San Francisco. We spent a week in Sedona, Arizona, and Tom didn't want to leave; actually, neither did I. We particularly loved our rides through the red rock mountains. The natural beauty and serenity of these mountains showered us with a peacefulness that was difficult to describe. Tom walked along scenic trails, waded in cold creeks, and swam in the hotel pool. I was in awe at his ability to do such normal things again. It felt like God had taken his hand and was gently leading him along a new path, at least for this trip.

It took three weeks to get home. We stopped in South Carolina to visit his sister Lois and her family. That reunion was a joyous event, and it relieved much of the worry that Lois had had about Tom for so long. Then we stopped in North Carolina to visit his older brother Eddie and his wife. Eddie had been the reason Tom had joined the navy, and they had a close relationship. Like everyone else in the family, they were thrilled to see Tom in such good health and enjoying life again.

After we got home, the peacefulness soon ended, and our life erupted into a new routine of ups and downs. It was discovered that the megadoses of steroids had affected his kidney function. He had occasional blood clots in his legs. Once, he was admitted to the hospital for "failure to thrive" because he had become so lethargic. He still suffered from lung infections in his remaining bad lung. He was hospitalized an average of once every three months.

It was a struggle to stay optimistic at times. A particularly bad time happened on our way home from one of those long days at the hospital. We had left early that morning for a series of tests. Once everything had been completed, we left the hospital during the evening rush hour. I was driving, tired and frustrated. The interstate south of Philadelphia was backed up with bumper-to-bumper cars. As we sat in traffic, Tom looked over and asked, "Are you okay?"

I looked back and said, "Do I have a choice?"

I instantly regretted what I had said. I apologized immediately. I knew that his feelings were hurt because he had told me several times how bad he felt that I had so much responsibility taking care of him. I apologized again. Even though he said he understood, the guilt I felt then was one of the worst feelings I had ever had. I vowed to have more patience.

"Do I have a choice?" Of course, I had a choice! I could have responded with more compassion and assured him that I was okay, or I could have said that I was tired and just anxious to get home. I could have said a dozen things, but instead, I lashed out at the most blameless person I knew. None of this was his fault; he was the one suffering through so many complications and endless trips to the hospital. Even though I recognized that my calloused and regrettable response was the result of my own frustration, tiredness, and inability to make his life better, it haunts me still.

Throughout all of these months, the paperwork continued back and forth with the Veterans Administration (VA). The professor and the law students at Widener Law School continued digging through Tom's military records, and they submitted new doctor reports that reflected his declining medical condition. Finally, the VA agreed that the war had caused Tom to have PTSD. And the stress from the PTSD had contributed to his heart attack. And his lungs had been affected by the heart attack. And the transplant had been necessary because of his bad lungs. He was eventually awarded a 60 percent disability pension. He was absolutely elated with the decision, and he was deeply grateful. It had been several years since he had filed his first claim.

After the VA approved Tom's disability pension, he was thankful that he would once again be contributing financially to our marriage. However, that was secondary to the fact that his military service had finally been validated. By awarding the disability claim, the government had acknowledged that Tom had made an enormous sacrifice for his country. For years, he had checked the mail every day to see if his claims had been approved, to see if his government had recognized how he was suffering. And for years, there had been nothing but silence and rejection.

However, the professor at Widener Law School was not satisfied with the government's response. He pointed out that the VA had used the wrong date to determine Tom's monthly benefit. Instead of using the date he was in Vietnam, they had used the date he had *originally* filed the claim. Unbelievable! Additionally, since Tom had been classified as *nonemployable*, and I had been assigned his fiduciary responsibilities, the professor said he should be classified as 100 percent disabled. We filed another appeal. I had very little confidence in the government's response, but there was no harm in trying.

In the meantime, Terri's sickness continued to worsen, and she lost more weight. She was extremely tired and vomiting every day. Her doctor referred her to the University of Pennsylvania Hospital in Philadelphia for additional testing. She was diagnosed with a rare blood disease that was affecting both her heart and digestive system. When I researched the disease, it was frightening to learn that few people survived for more than a year when their heart was affected.

Soon, I was making regular trips to Philadelphia again as I took Terri for checkups. After a few weeks of tests, her doctor recommended a stem cell transplant as her only hope for survival. She was ten years younger than me, and she had never had any health concerns. Her diagnosis—and especially her prognosis—came as a shock. I struggled to grasp the cruelty of it all.

Much like Tom, Terri had to go through several other tests to determine if she was strong enough to have the surgery. After she was approved, I arranged for Lois to come and stay with Tom while I stayed with Terri at the hospital. The surgery was successful, but she had to stay in the hospital for several days, so I stayed at a nearby hotel. Her husband's health had been failing, and he was unable to make the trip. Besides, I knew she wanted me to be there with her.

As I sat at her bedside, Terri and I had long conversations, reminiscing. We laughed and talked about how important it had been to paint that fence long ago. Those days we had spent talking in between the wooden fence stakes had been a turning point in our friendship. We had shared so many of our own individual experiences and what we had learned from them. We had talked about our beliefs and values and expectations in life, and a deep feeling of mutual respect had developed.

I reminded her of the trip to Atlantic City when we had taken part of our fence earnings to go play the slot machines. While driving there, we had passed a large farmhouse trimmed in white Christmas lights. I told her that I thought white lights were boring; we had always had colored Christmas lights when I was growing up. She thought the white lights were elegant; she had grown up with white lights. We had argued about it for quite a while on the way home that night. But that very next Christmas, I trimmed my home in white lights, and she decorated hers with colored lights. That was just one instance when we were able to acknowledge the value in the other's viewpoint and subsequently change our own opinions. It was this kind of mutual respect that had become the foundation of our friendship. And we had laughed about it many times over the years.

We recalled the significance of opening our business after she had abruptly quit her job. We laughed about the time we had taken a long bus trip to hear the country band Alabama play at a state fair. The concert was canceled because of a strong thunderstorm, and we had a miserable ride home in soaking wet clothes. We laughed about that time we had decided to drive to the amusement park in New Jersey, where we had stopped at a restaurant/bar for lunch, spent the day shooting darts and drinking beer, and never made it to the park! We laughed about all the adventures of meeting so many different kinds of people throughout the years that we had been in business together. I have often thought that all that laughter in the hospital had been the best medicine for her. I know it was for me.

The stem cell transplant worked well for Terri, and she was soon back to feeling almost normal. It was wonderful to see her be her upbeat self again. It was a good thing too because she was faced with challenges at home as Roy's health declined. He had become quite demanding and irritable. Terri's mother's health was also deteriorating. She was not able to live alone, so she moved in with Terri and Roy.

This was a year filled with health problems. That winter, Dad fell and broke his hip. He was walking out to his workshop when he slipped on a patch of ice. His recovery was long and slow, and we made numerous trips home to visit him. He became quite discouraged because he was unable to do much of anything. The long winter months of being homebound took a toll on his mental health as well.

Dad also had COPD. His diagnosis was the result of a lifetime of smoking and exposure to numerous respiratory irritants in the lumber business. He had begun smoking during the war, where there had always been a plentiful supply of cigarettes. Over the last few years, he had eliminated cigarettes, but he was still smoking a pipe. He said it was one of the few pleasures he had left.

Dad loved telling stories about World War II. He had been an aircraft mechanic stationed in the Philippines, and he often flew on missions. His favorite story was when General MacArthur came to headquarters on the island. Like cigarettes, there was always an abundance of beer on base. Because it was stored in warehouses, the beer was always hot. Each time, before the general arrived, Dad said they were told to load the beer onto a plane, take off, circle at several thousand feet until the beer got cold, and then deliver it to headquarters up on the hill. He would laugh and say, "I bet you never read about that in the history books!"

In addition to the war stories, Dad talked a lot about his hunting experiences as a young boy. His mother used to rent out rooms to hunters during deer season. After the hunters shot deer, they would drag them out of the woods and leave them at the bottom of the hill by the railroad tracks. Dad told us about how he and his younger brother used to drag the dead deer, sometimes a mile or more, on the railroad tracks to get back to their house, where the hunters would give them five cents for each deer! He loved an audience, and so many times, the kitchen was full of family laughing at his childhood antics.

Soon, Dad began to have serious lung infections. My heart ached as I watched him slowly decline. His quality of life deteriorated, and he often said he was ready to die, noting, "Dying is part of living."

It was a hot summer day when my sister Kathy called and said Dad was not doing well again. He had been in the local hospital for what appeared to be another typical lung infection. Several times, he would spend a few days in the hospital, only to be discharged and sent home, but this time was different. Tom and I immediately packed a bag and started the drive to the hospital. We were about halfway there when Kathy called. Dad was gone.

I pulled off the side of the road and cried my heart out. I wanted to be with him to say goodbye. Once again, Tom was by my side, and I knew he felt the same pain that I felt.

The next few days were the same as when Mom had died. There was the flurry of friends who stopped by, food and flowers delivered, and a house full of family—kids, grandkids, and great-grandkids. As I had done when Mom died, I drove to the crematory after the funeral, and I watched Dad be cremated. Not all of my siblings went with me, but it was something I needed to do.

"Ashes to ashes, dust to dust" was a phrase I had heard many times. Every life must come to an end. When I had heard that as a child, it frightened me. But I had learned that the phrase simply honors the cycle of life. Returning to ashes means that even though our body is gone, our soul continues on to heaven where there is only love. Watching Mom and Dad return to ashes did not eliminate my deep sadness. It did not fill the tremendous void in my life. It did not reduce the flow of tears. It simply brought me a sense of peace, knowing they were home with God.

In addition to my deep sadness, I felt something different now because I no longer had any parents. Would there be any *glue* to hold the family together? All the dozens of yearly trips "back home" were no longer needed. This loss not only broke my heart; it also forced me to look at my own mortality.

*****

I lingered at this hovering spot with such a sense of gratitude for the blessings God continued to shower upon my life. Tom's lung transplant surgery had been two years ago, which was more years than we had once thought possible. Even with the numerous complications and his difficult, frightening hospitalizations, he was grateful to be alive. He lived to see the birth of two new grandchildren. We took a six-week trip across the country and saw sights he never expected to see. He walked on beaches and hiked through mountains. He attended weddings, graduations, birthday parties, and holiday dinners. He lived to see the Veterans Administration finally acknowledge his sacrifice during the Vietnam War. And seldom a day went by when he didn't openly express his indebtedness to the young man who had died and donated his lung.

As for me, my life had undergone a drastic transformation as a full-time caregiver. The career I had loved so much now felt far behind me, and I was a different person. Early retirement was not a decision I would have made if Tom had not been so sick. Now I was faced with new daily challenges of managing medical symptoms, monitoring drug interactions, and traveling to emergency rooms, hospitals, labs, clinics, and doctors' offices. Even with the grueling responsibilities of managing Tom's health, I was extremely grateful to have had the chance to continue making memories with the love of my life.

Death was more prevalent during these years. Both my sister Betty Ann and Terri lost their spouses. They now faced what I secretly feared the most—losing my life's partner and facing an unknown future alone.

I had watched Dad struggle with the challenges of caregiving and the pain of loss after Mom died, and now, Dad's death had brought a deeper sense of sadness. I had also lost my dear aunt Marty. She had been such a factor in my choosing to join the air force.

Yes, I recognized that those whom I had loved so much were at peace and home with God, but that dreaded finality of death and the dark void left behind still frightened me. Death is not a singular event. With it comes the death of hopes and dreams and expectations for the future.

*****

Reflections

1. Caregiving duties range from the mundane tasks of bathing and feeding to medical triage. How have you experienced any of these emotional and spiritual challenges? If you have not yet experienced caregiving, how might you prepare yourself for such a responsibility?

   _____
   _____
   _____
   _____

2. Transformative change means doing things differently from how we are used to doing them. What life event has dramatically transformed your life? Think about how you dealt with the change. How did that change actually change you?

   _____
   _____
   _____
   _____

3. We have the power to change our perspective in any situation by choosing how we want to look at it. Is there a situation in your life right now that you can improve simply by looking at it differently? Please explain.

   _____
   _____
   _____
   _____

CHAPTER 11

Unexpected Results

Tom loved hot weather and the outdoors. He enjoyed rides through the countryside, and he particularly liked to sit on our backyard deck and savor the peacefulness of the trees and flowers. The cold, dreary days and long, dark evenings of winter were difficult for him. He lost his taste for food and became thin and pale. He had always been a large man with a good appetite, so this was unusual, and I was concerned.

Although he never talked about it, I knew his thoughts of death were becoming more frequent. The last couple of hospitalizations had also dampened his spirits. On the way home from one of them, he said, "I'm getting tired of all of this." But always at some of his most discouraged moments, he would say, "I don't want to leave you."

I always smiled and reassured him by saying, "Tomorrow will be a better day."

Then he would smile back and say, "I love you."

This routine was happening more and more often lately.

It had been particularly upsetting to him when his cognitive skills declined. It wasn't long before the doctor recommended that Tom quit driving. Losing that independence was a turning point for him. He was also losing hope.

I knew exactly what he meant when he said that he was getting tired of everything. It had been over four years since the transplant surgery, and he had been hospitalized over twenty times. It had been twelve years since his heart attack, and for several of those years, he had been on oxygen twenty-four hours a day. We had made over 225 trips to Temple Hospital in Philadelphia. It was indeed tiring.

I got quite concerned about the number of drugs he took every day. In addition to the transplant drugs, he was still on medications the VA doctors had prescribed for PTSD and pain from a back injury he sustained while in the navy.

At the height of his illness, he took almost sixty pills a day. These ranged from normal vitamin supplements to powerful immunosuppressants. I had reviewed the list of drugs with the doctors many times to see if any could be reduced or removed. They periodically tried to modify different ones, but they were never able to permanently eliminate any.

One day after he got home from one of his hospitalizations, Tom slipped in the kitchen and broke his shoulder. Even for a broken bone, he had to go back to Temple Hospital for treatment. On another occasion, he was hospitalized for severe constipation, which was a side effect of his pain medication. It was a vicious circle.

On yet another occasion, Tom got extremely sick with abdominal pain and severe diarrhea. He spent over a week in intensive care and then another several days in the pulmonary ward. That sickness was caused by a common virus, cytomegalovirus (CMV), that was present in the new lung he had received during the transplant surgery. Although the presence of the virus had been a concern for the doctors, they explained that it was worth the risk, as without the new lung, he would die.

The doctor explained to us how a healthy person's immune system usually keeps this virus under control. However, because the transplant had compromised Tom's immune system, he contracted the virus and became seriously ill. A powerful drug used to counteract the virus was now added to his daily medication regimen. I read the possible side effects, and they included kidney damage, low blood cell counts, harmful to bone marrow, and "can cause cancer." These side effects were more foreboding than those of any of his other drugs, and I shuddered.

Tom's most recent hospitalization was due to poor kidney function. For several months after the transplant, he had been on large doses of steroids. The steroids, along with an antirejection drug and a diuretic, all affected kidney function. When his kidney function reached a critically low level, he was referred to a nephrologist. The recommendation was to insert a fistula in his arm in preparation for dialysis. This is a surgical procedure where a blood vessel is made wider and stronger to handle the needles used with a dialysis machine. Tom had the procedure done, but it did not work properly. When the doctor suggested that it be performed again, Tom said, "No more."

The nephrologist further reviewed his medications and replaced one of the antirejection drugs. His kidney function improved enough to not warrant the fistula. Again, it was all such a vicious circle.

One morning at the kitchen table, we talked about the overwhelming number of doctors and the unending tests and procedures. For every new doctor whom Tom saw, there was a new diagnosis or medical concern of some kind. Using my record of visits, we made a list of everyone he had seen since his surgery. When I finished the list, we looked at each other in pure amazement. The list included transplant surgeons and nurses, a cardiologist, pulmonologist, psychologist, psychiatrist, nephrologist, chiropractor, gastroenterologist, urologist, podiatrist, orthopedist, ophthalmologist, MRI/CT technologists, X-ray and lab technicians, physical therapists, home-care nurses, paramedics, and our primary-care doctor.

Additionally, with each hospitalization, we were required to complete the same paperwork at the admittance office. For every new doctor he visited, we were asked the same questions over again. I always kept multiple updated copies of his medication list with me because every medical visit required one. It was mind-boggling. We decided that from now on, he would only see the transplant doctors and our family doctor.

I thought of what they had told us about Tom's health during the initial transplant evaluation process. "Tom may trade one thing for another because of the complexity of the medications." At the time, we just nodded and said we understood. However, over the past four years, we had learned that we actually had no idea what they had meant. Tom was angry. He said if he had understood then, he would not have had the surgery. I knew that wasn't true, but it showed his level of frustration.

After the holidays, the long winter months ahead felt daunting, so we decided to travel to warmer weather for the month of February. We rented a house in Florida near the Gulf of Mexico, and we enthusiastically packed our suitcases with summer clothes and headed south.

Much like our cross-country trip a few years earlier, it was precisely the right decision. We were comfortable in the rental. It was a private home located in a quiet neighborhood and on a canal only several yards from the back porch. It had a small heated indoor swimming pool that was especially relaxing. The weather was warm and sunny every day, and the evenings were delightfully cool as we walked around the neighborhood each evening. We spent most afternoons on the beach.

The blue waters of the Gulf reminded me of my days in Florida. I thought about the time Tom had come to visit me when he was on military leave. He had acted like such a different person then, so quiet, so somber. We had decided to part as friends, but we eventually lost touch completely. Now here we were, sitting on the beach together not far from that same base where we had parted over forty years ago. Surely, God had a hand in this!

Now, all these years later, I understood why he had been so quiet and somber back then. The innocent, jovial guy I had known in high school had seen the horrors of war. He had even felt guilty about being frightened...in a jungle where people were killed every day!

Once again, I felt pangs of humiliation as I remembered my immaturity in getting married to Brian. My naive childhood had been filled with simple times and a loving home, and I was thankful for that solid foundation. But it had definitely left me unprepared for the *real* world. My exposure to the dysfunctional family stories in the military, my abusive marriage, and Tom's post-traumatic stress disorder were all eye-openers to a world I never knew existed.

But that was then, and this was now. Despite the choices we had made and the experiences that had created who we were, God had given us the opportunity to close the circle of our lives together. Tom still suffered in many ways, and I was convinced that God knew I was the best one to take care of him.

Although Tom's appetite had not returned completely, he was happy to eat dinners at restaurants where we sat outside and gazed in awe of the sunsets. Each evening after dinner, he reached across the table, touched my hand, smiled, and said, "Life is good."

One morning at breakfast, I noticed what looked like a small pool of blood under the skin on Tom's face. I asked him if he had cut himself while shaving, but he said he hadn't. I was constantly on the lookout for something unusual because I had learned, sometimes the hard way, that the smallest of things could be an indication of something worse to come. I shrugged it off, but I kept an eye on it, and it disappeared in a few days.

We hated to see our month of summer weather come to an end. It had been a very relaxing time away from the daily routines at home, and the warm sunshine had definitely lifted our spirits. The drive down had been exciting as we looked forward to a change of pace. The drive home felt much longer, but at least we had a month of winter behind us. March brought the first signs of spring and a fresh outlook.

After getting Tom settled at home, I went to visit Terri, and I was shocked at her appearance. She had lost more weight, and she was vomiting again almost daily. She hadn't told me that when I had called her from Florida. I took her to the hospital for her monthly checkup, and it was not good news. Her blood work indicated her disease had returned, and the doctor wanted to start chemotherapy treatments immediately.

She had to have the first couple of treatments at the hospital in Philadelphia. She was tired and weak, and the trip was difficult for her. Many times, as I pushed her down the long hallways in a wheelchair, I fought back tears. I wasn't sure what was ahead, and it frightened me.

UNEXPECTED RESULTS

This was a different hospital than the one Tom went to, but the hallways looked the same. Pictures of past doctors who had pioneered the cure for many diseases. And here I was again, noticing their eyes watching us and wondering why there was no cure for what Terri had.

These were grueling days. I often wondered if God wasn't getting tired of my praying for the same thing day after day—better health and hope for Tom and Terri, strength and guidance for me. There are only so many ways you can ask for the same thing, and I hoped God had patience with me.

I could feel myself slipping into depression. The transplant nurses had already told me that my attention to detail was keeping Tom alive. But recently, I felt as though I was losing my confidence as I tried to take care of both Tom and Terri.

I knew the sheer exhaustion contributed to my feeling of inadequacy, but I also knew I had to do better with Terri. That inevitable void left after her husband's death had created an unexpected loneliness in her life. While she still had many friends, I knew she wished we could spend more time together.

She often said, "I miss you," but then she hurriedly followed it by saying how she understood my situation at home. On one hand, I wished for more hours in the day; on the other hand, I struggled to get through the daily demands of each one.

There was rarely a Sunday when Tom and I missed going to church. Our faith was deep, and we believed in the power of prayer. We often talked about God's love and how grateful we were to be together again. We recognized how painful some of the past had been, but we also knew those years apart had been the result of choices we had made. It was important now to focus on our time together and to enjoy the depth of our love.

Pastor Mary and our church family became very important to us. Mary Lou and Kathy were two retired nurses who usually came and talked to us after church. They showed a genuine concern for Tom, and they asked him plenty of questions. He was touched by their sincerity, and I appreciated the attention they gave him.

Pastor Mary stayed in touch with me. After spending the night with Tom at the local emergency room one night, I called her at 6:00 a.m. to let her know that he was very sick again. Within minutes, she arrived and prayed for us. More and more as time went by, I needed to hear her prayers. She mentioned our names when she asked God for guidance and strength. I used to say basically the same prayer, but hearing our names out loud added a new dimension. As she held our hands, I felt the warmth of her touch, and I felt closer to God.

There was another woman in church, Linda, who always waved and smiled. She sent several cards to let us know she was praying for us. One day, she called and asked if I would like to meet her for lunch. We set a date, but then I was unable to go because Tom was hospitalized again. I heard from her several more times, but I simply didn't have the strength to socialize.

As the days went by, the weather was warmer, daylight hours lasted longer, and it felt good to be outside again. Each year, we had more and more plants and flowers blooming from early spring to late autumn. I worked many long hours in the yard, and I enjoyed every minute. I found myself breathing more deeply and appreciating the natural world as I worked in the soil. It was especially amusing as I trimmed off the larger flower blossoms only to find smaller, younger ones beneath them, patiently waiting for their share of daylight and sunshine! It soothed my soul. Tom said it felt like "heaven on earth" as we sat on the deck and admired the red rose bushes, the multi-colored coneflowers, and the bright-white daises with their yellow centers. It bothered him that he couldn't work in the yard due to potentially dangerous exposures to bacteria and mold.

It wasn't long before I noticed another small red spot on Tom's face. Like the one I had noticed when we were on vacation, it was just a small pool of blood under his skin. There was neither soreness nor warmth to it, so I was puzzled. Fortunately, he had a routine checkup the following week, so I decided to wait and point it out to the doctor then.

Everything appeared to be stable with Tom's health during the checkup, but because of those small red spots on his skin, the doctor ordered additional blood work to rule out any type of disease or infection. A few days later, she called and asked us to return to Temple Hospital for a consultation.

The blood work had come back with some abnormal results, and the doctor wanted Tom to see a hematologist. Since we had recently decided not to see any more doctors, Tom looked at me questioningly. I knew this decision was going to be left entirely up to me, and I felt a wave of absolute fatigue slowly expand throughout my body.

The doctor understood our reluctance. She was well aware of Tom's complications, hospitalizations, and the years of grueling trips to the hospital. She said she thought Tom should at least have the initial hematology visit and explained that it was only to rule out any further indication of blood disease. Blood disease? That was a term I had never heard any of his doctors mention before. The only research I had done on blood disease was after Terri had been diagnosed. My fatigue was instantly replaced with fear. Tom had a faraway look on his face, but I agreed to bring him back for the visit.

Once back home, Tom's mood became even more solemn. He sat for hours without talking. He paid no attention to what he watched on television. When I took him out for our countryside rides, he often fell asleep. He sat on the deck in silence.

One evening, he sat with me at the kitchen table while I filled his pillbox. I wanted him to take more responsibility for taking pills on his own. Usually, I just handed them to him, but I was worried that I was enabling him to become more and more dependent upon me. I didn't want him to lose any more of his independence.

When I was finished, I closed the pillbox lid and looked across the table at him. His eyes were filled with the tender innocence of a child. As we looked at each other, he said nothing. He didn't have to. I knew at that moment, he had surrendered. Without speaking, his eyes told me that I was completely in charge from now on. It broke my heart.

I gave in to a feeling of complete *aloneness*. I walked outside late one evening and nearly collapsed. I didn't know what was happening. Or maybe I didn't want to know what was happening. I tried to reason with God.

I still didn't understand *why* all the side effects, complications, and hospitalizations kept happening to Tom, and that was okay for a while. I didn't need to understand *why* Tom might be facing another serious disease. Right now, I wanted to know *what* God was going to do about it. Tom had suffered enough, and I was tired.

Sure, Tom had had plenty of good days during the past five years. He had been able to watch the kids grow, get married to wonderful spouses, and have children of their own. He had experienced two perfect vacations, and he had seen sights he never dreamed of visiting. He had survived the war.

After his heart attack, he had dragged oxygen tanks around with him for seven years. Since the lung transplant, he had struggled with over twenty hospitalizations. Doesn't he deserve some peace?

I was scared when I saw that first red spot on his face while we were vacationing in Florida. Now it was developing into…what? A blood disease? What do we do now?

I had agonized over managing his ever-changing medications for all these years. I had spent days and nights pouring over medication documentation and keeping meticulous records that the doctors used to help determine treatments and next steps. I had learned to give him daily insulin shots. I had learned to give shots of Lovenox in his stomach when he had blood clots. I had made dozens of exhausting trips to the hospital. I had called 911 three different times. I had watched a helicopter whisk him away. I had followed the ambulance to Philadelphia, drenched in sheer anxiety and praying all the way. So haven't I earned some peace too?

I sat very still, but there were no answers. I knew how tired and frightened I felt. I tried to comprehend how Tom felt. I couldn't.

It was May, and the weather was beautiful. I made sure Tom was outside every day. We did all of his favorite things—took long rides, stopped for ice cream cones, sat on our deck and held hands, walked on the boardwalk at the beach. We watched silly movies, but now that much-loved belly laugh was missing again. I tried to keep the days filled with activities so that neither one of us would think too much.

UNEXPECTED RESULTS

During the month, more of those red spots appeared on Tom's face and also on his arms. We went to the hematology appointment, and he had extensive blood work done. The doctor called a few days later and wanted to review the results with us, so we were off to the hospital again.

His blood work indicated the presence of a rare form of cancer that typically progresses into leukemia. Tom needed to start chemotherapy treatments as soon as possible. The doctor scheduled the first round for early June.

We drove home in silence. Neither one of us could think of anything to say. Always, in the past, when we had received troubling news, one of us had been able to stay positive. That wasn't the case this time. This was not just another "bump in the road" or another "hill to climb" or another "storm before the calm." This was more than either one of us could talk about.

The cancer center was located about ten miles north of Temple Hospital, so that meant more traffic and a longer drive. It also meant another new doctor's office, new nurses and technicians, more questions, and the ever-changing medication list. Now I needed to track chemotherapy treatments as well as additional lab results.

Trips to the lab for blood work happened more frequently. The doctors were now tracking his white blood cell count, particularly a type called neutrophils, which helped heal damaged tissues and infections. I learned what the healthy limit was within the body. If Tom's neutrophil count was too low, it was risky to have a chemo treatment. I regularly received copies of the blood work, so I always knew what to expect whenever the nurse called with the results.

Anytime Tom required overnight testing at Temple Hospital, we stayed at the Gift of Life family house in downtown Philadelphia. It was considered a "home away from home" for transplant patients and their families, and it provided temporary living and support services. It was a wonderful relief to not have to stay in a hotel as I had done for the first year after his surgery. It had a warm and caring atmosphere that made us feel like we were staying with family or friends. Home-cooked meals were provided every evening by volunteers from the area. The entire staff and the other transplant patients and their families were some of the most compassionate people I had ever met.

Staying at this facility improved Tom's attitude because he was able to talk to other patients who were going through some of the same complications he had endured. Every patient who stayed there was involved in some phase of a transplant. Some were just beginning the evaluation process, so we were able to tell them what things to expect. The ages of the patients ranged from small children to elderly adults. Many needed lungs, but others needed kidneys or a heart. Everyone shared feelings of apprehension and anxiety, but there were also desperate feelings of hope. God was definitely a permanent resident of that beloved home away from home.

Tom was to receive a daily dose of chemo for five days every month. After the initial round, his blood work showed a sharp drop in the level of neutrophils. Although that was expected, the count remained low. The second round of chemo was canceled to allow time for him to receive both blood and platelet transfusions. Thankfully, he was able to get the transfusions at the local hospital.

He was finally able to receive the second round of chemo treatments, again followed by weekly blood and platelet transfusions. These procedures could take hours. We waited a particularly long time once when the local supply of platelets had been depleted, and units had to be delivered from another town. I had always been a volunteer blood donor, but I had never been aware of the need for platelets. This firsthand experience gave me a better perspective on their importance.

Once again, the third round of chemo also had to be rescheduled to allow a healthy blood count to return. The doctor was concerned about the elapsed time between treatments, but it was too risky to proceed prematurely. This added another layer of anxiety on top of what we were already experiencing.

After two more transfusions, Tom's blood count was *borderline*. The doctor told us there was a degree of risk for the chemo treatment, but he left the decision up to us. Tom did not want to wait any longer. He was getting weaker, and he had lost more weight. I knew he just wanted to get the treatment over with. I emphasized the risk that the doctor talked about, but Tom's eyes were pleading for me to agree with him.

I reserved another five days at the Gift of Life House, and we went to Philadelphia. The first two days of treatments went well. Tom was mentally energized, but he was still very tired and weak. After dinner on the second day, he didn't want to stay downstairs and talk to anyone. This was unusual for him because he truly enjoyed talking to the other patients.

When we returned after the third day of treatment, he was acting strangely. I had to help him out of the truck, and he was too tired to walk to our room. I guided him out to the patio and found a table with chairs. Thinking he needed some food, I went to the kitchen to fix some lunch. When I came back to the table, he was crying. I felt numb. "What's the matter, sweetheart?" I asked.

He looked at me and said, "I'm dying, and I don't want to leave you."

I cradled him in my arms and tried to reassure him just as I had done so many times before. Only this time, I cried with him.

We managed to slowly walk to our room and lie down on the bed. As I held him, I could feel his arms and face getting hot, and I knew he had a fever. I went down to the front desk and explained the situation to the night-shift clerk, and she immediately called 911.

For the third time in five years, I felt like I was watching a movie. The ambulance arrived, and the paramedics placed Tom on a stretcher and wheeled him outside. I got in the truck, and within seconds, I was careening through downtown traffic, nervously driving through red lights, and following the ambulance as closely as I could. When we arrived at the emergency room, Tom was rushed in and surrounded by a swarm of doctors and nurses.

After a few hours, he was moved to the intensive care unit. He had a raging lung infection. He was monitored for a few days, but the doctors were unable to control the infection. I stayed by his side, encouraging him as much as I could and hanging on every word the doctors said.

Two days later, he was moved to the pulmonary ward even though he wasn't any better. The nurse told me it was "too dangerous" for him to stay in the intensive care unit.

I called Andy and Michelle, Terri, Tom's two sisters, and Pastor Mary. Lois flew in from South Carolina, and I picked her up at the airport the next day. We stayed with him all night, but he never woke up.

Pastor Mary arrived in the morning as I was talking to the doctor. He told me that the only recourse now was for Tom to have a bronchoscopy, but he also said he couldn't guarantee it would be of any help in further diagnosis since the infection was so intense and widespread.

Out of the barrage of tests and procedures Tom had tolerated over the years, he absolutely detested a bronchoscopy the most. It involved passing a thin tube through his nose or mouth, down through his throat, and into his lungs.

For the past couple of years, Pastor Mary had watched Tom suffer repeatedly through complications, bounce back, and then slowly decline again. She had told me more than once that I should think about "letting go." I realized she knew more about death and dying than I did, but whenever she had mentioned it in the past, I simply wouldn't consider it. This time, when she said it, the doctor agreed.

Everyone left the room while I talked to Tom. Even though I knew he couldn't respond, I talked to him about the bronchoscopy. I told him how I knew he hated the procedure more than anything else he had endured. I told him the doctor wasn't even sure if the bronchoscopy would help them decide how to treat the infection. I told him Lois was here to be with him. I told him Pastor Mary was here praying for him. I told him the kids were waiting to see him. I told him I loved him.

It was about 11:00 a.m., and I decided to take him home. I called the Delaware Hospice organization to see if they could deliver a hospital bed to our home. Once I explained the situation, they asked for our address and said there would be a bed there by 4:00 p.m. Terri was going to let them in since I wasn't sure when we would get there.

UNEXPECTED RESULTS

Once I made that decision, the transplant doctor and nurses stopped by his room to say goodbye. I didn't know how to properly thank them for all they had done over the years. Tom had always teased them relentlessly about their poking and prodding during his checkups. They remembered the year he had been hospitalized on his birthday, and how we had all shared a cake and sang to him. They remembered that huge box of Ghirardelli chocolate we had sent to them from San Francisco while on our cross-country trip. They loved Tom and his fighting attitude.

Lois and I followed the ambulance out of the city, and when we arrived at home, Terri was there with the hospice people. The hospital bed had been set up in the living room. Michelle was on her way, Lois helped the nurse get Tom situated in bed, and Pastor Mary took a prescription for morphine to the local pharmacy.

I continued to watch the movie. The hospice nurse stayed for quite a while. Lois wrote down instructions for when to give Tom morphine and what signs to look for as he began "actively dying." Actively dying—I had never heard those words before.

By the end of the evening, it was just Tom, Lois, and I in the living room. Tom never regained consciousness from the time he was moved from intensive care to the pulmonary ward. However, I was hoping he now knew he was home and would wake up during the night.

Even though we had both been up since the previous morning, Lois kept busy around the house while I sat with Tom. She came in and out of the living room throughout the night. We talked about what a blessing it was that Tom had called me so many years ago. She told me that even though we had been separated for twenty-five years, he had never stopped loving me.

Tom and Lois had a very special bond, and he used to tell me silly stories about when they were growing up. He also loved his older sister MaryAnne. Tom had lived with her during some of his darkest years after the war. His brother Eddie had died very unexpectedly just eight months ago.

The hours ticked by as I downloaded some of our favorite love songs to my phone. While holding his swollen hand, I laid my phone on his chest and played "Unchained Melody" again and again.

I didn't feel tired anymore. I felt God's presence fill the room, and I knew Tom felt it too. As the songs softly played, I told him that it was okay to let go. I told him he had done such a wonderful job with all of his projects and how pretty our home looked. I told him Terri had been feeling better lately, and she had been here to see him. I told him the kids kept calling to see how he was doing. I told him that we didn't have many bills, and that I would be okay financially. I told him that I would continue to fight with the VA until he got 100 percent disability.

I told him it was okay to leave me. I could never have found that kind of strength on my own. I sensed God knew the enormous scope of sadness in this room. I knew God was sad too. I didn't cry as I talked to Tom. I was confident and reassuring. I told him he had been too sick for too long, and it was time to be home with God. I told him his mom and dad and brother were all anxious to see him. I asked him to give my mom and dad a hug for me.

Daylight came, and the hospice nurse returned. A hospice pastor also stopped by. Both Terri and Pastor Mary arrived a little later. It was a warm and sunny day, and Lois suggested that I go outside for some fresh air. Pastor Mary and I walked out to the backyard and sat on the swing.

Just as we sat down, Lois called my name and said, "Hurry up!"

I went running back into the house only to find Tom gone. Lois said as soon as I walked out, Tom opened his eyes for a split second and then died. She said she was sure he knew he was leaving, and he didn't want me to be there at that instant.

*****

I did not hover over this part of my virtual tour. I literally stopped. I felt as though I had hit the ground, and I simply couldn't take it all in again. Stepping back now and looking at those years from a distance didn't make it feel any less real. My heart simply broke again. I thought, *How did Tom do it? How did he keep going for all those years?*

We used to talk about how he was not only a transplant patient but also a "research project." Given Tom's complicated history, doctors were often unsure about what medications to prescribe, which procedures to perform. We knew that future patients would benefit from whatever the doctors learned through their experiences with Tom. He always said this was his way of "giving back" for the lung that had given us more precious years together.

I couldn't help but think back over the sequence of events. The war caused him to suffer from PTSD, and that caused him to have a heart attack. The heart attack damaged his lungs so badly that they needed to be replaced. The lung that he received had a common virus that typically doesn't result in any health issues, but the transplant had compromised his immune system. As a result, he became very ill, and a powerful drug was prescribed to counteract that virus. One of the stated side effects of the drug was that it could cause cancer, and Tom died of leukemia.

How did he do it? How did he keep going for all those years? It was our love that kept him going. It was our love that kept me going. We had fallen in love in high school; it was fun and exciting then. That same love had resurfaced twenty-five years later, and it formed a foundation that was unshakeable.

The impact of these rippling events had felt like waves that kept growing and expanding…until now, when it suddenly felt like there was nothing left.

*****

Reflections

1. The loss of a loved one grabs our heart and doesn't let go. It can wound and paralyze us because love and loss are deeply related. If you have lost someone, have you realized a level of love found only in your loss? Please explain.

   _____
   _____
   _____
   _____

2. The trials that we face don't need to be roadblocks. Through perseverance and hope, we can move forward and treat them as detours. Name a challenge that you treated as a roadblock. Name a challenge that you treated as a detour. Which one made you stronger? Why or why not?

   _____
   _____
   _____
   _____

3. The choices we make, no matter how small, can lead to much-bigger changes than we could have ever imagined. What are some choices you have made that have had an unexpected impact on your life? On the life of another?

   _____
   _____
   _____
   _____

CHAPTER 12

The Aftermath

Tom was gone. The movie continued as I watched friends and family stop by. Andy flew in from Oregon. Flowers were delivered, and the kitchen table was overflowing with food that had been dropped off. I thought about how I had watched the same events unfold after Mom—and then Dad—had died. Now I was living it all over again.

Pastor Mary and I talked about funeral arrangements. She was traveling out of the country shortly, so we planned a memorial service to be held at the church in mid-October, about three weeks away. Andy went to the funeral home with me to take care of more details. I was under a fog-like numbness, and nothing felt real. Perhaps that was God's way of protecting me from the pain of such a loss.

As I looked around the house, I saw Tom everywhere. What should I do with the half-filled pillbox? What about his cane and walker and wheelchair? What about his jacket on the back of the chair? What about his toothbrush in the bathroom and his slippers by the bed? *What about me?*

Cards arrived daily, and there were plenty of phone calls, but Tom was gone. His words, "I don't want to leave you," kept running through my mind, and each time, I felt my heart crack a little more.

Pastor Mary reminded me that there is no concept of time in heaven. She said, "When Tom turns around, you will be there." Those were very comforting words. All the cards were full of comforting words, but after the words were spoken, the cards were opened, and everyone went home, the deafening silence bounced off the walls. It echoed down the hallway and lurked in every corner of the house. It followed me everywhere I went.

My mind struggled to process a whirlpool of emotions. I suddenly realized that when I had tried to comfort Terri in her time of grief after the loss of her husband, I truly had no idea how she felt. I now understood that the incomprehensible pain of losing a spouse can only be felt when you actually go through it yourself. But as Terri had told me, everyone's circumstance is different, and each of us grieves in our own way and in our own time.

So maybe everyone's circumstance is different, and maybe everyone grieves in her own way and in her own time, but I didn't want to grieve at all. I was angry. What did leukemia have to do with a lung transplant? I looked at Tom's death certificate. It stated eight causes of death—eight! There was an immediate cause. Then there were three causes contributing to the immediate cause (one of which was labeled the "underlying cause"). And then there were four "significant conditions" contributing to his death, one of which was "lung transplant." And under "Manner of Death," the box labeled "Natural" was checked. To me, there was nothing *natural* about his death or any of the medical complications of the past five years.

Shortly after he died, I received a certificate in the mail signed by the president of the United States, honoring Tom. It was from "a grateful nation in recognition of devoted and selfless consecration to the service of our country." Really? A grateful nation? A nation whose multiple presidents had lied to the public and sent him and thousands of others to a senseless war? A nation that had rejected him in such cruel ways when he returned home from that war? A grateful nation that had rejected his pleas for help for years? When I visited Tom at the cemetery, I apologized to him from our "grateful nation."

I wrestled with questions that had no answers. I didn't understand *why* Tom had died the way he did, or *why* he had to suffer so much only to die of a disease caused by a drug. It made no sense. And *why* was I now left alone?

I thought about when we were kids growing up near that old oil pumping station. When the oil fields dried up, the old pipes that were once filled and flowing with oil were then empty and unattended. We used to gather big sticks to pound on the pipes to see who could make the loudest noise and the longest echo. At first, the echo was so loud that it stung our ears. But as it traveled down the hollow pipe, it became softer until we could hardly hear it at all. Now I thought how that old pipe reminded me of my heart. Once vibrant and full of life, it was now empty and silent as the memory of Tom echoed through it. I wondered if it would get softer as it traveled through time.

I had been a single mother and a business owner for years, and those years demanded shuffling priorities, organizing busy schedules, meeting unrealistic deadlines, and raising children. But those days were gone now. The kids were gone, grown and active with their own lives and families. I had retired from a successful and rewarding career to take care of Tom; my job was gone. There were no more seemingly endless days of doctor visits, tests, procedures, trips to the hospitals and pharmacies. Tom was gone. My identity was gone. Who was I? What do I do now? Of course, there were no answers.

Tom's memorial service at the church was a great tribute to him. Our immediate family gathered upstairs in the church prior to the service to pray with Pastor Mary. Andy and Michelle told our three little grandsons that Papa Tom was in heaven. It was so touching as they each tried to hold my hand as we walked into the sanctuary. The church was filled with most of the same people who had helped us celebrate our wedding. Pastor Mary spoke of Tom's courage as he served our country during war and then fought valiantly through so many years with the challenges related to his illness. I'm sure Tom was smiling as everyone sang the last song at the service—"God Bless America."

After the church service, there was a navy color guard waiting for us at the cemetery. They gave the customary gun salute, played the military "Taps" song, and presented me with an American flag. As the two young sailors ceremoniously folded the flag in front of me, I could hear nothing but my heartbeat. It was slow and steady, as if I wanted this moment to last forever. I knew that once they handed me the flag and the service was over, my life would never be the same.

Everyone gathered at the house when we got back from the cemetery—all of Tom's family, all of my family, our church family, friends from years gone by. The house was full of people and laughter as they each told their own funny stories about Tom. I thought of the party we had had the night before our wedding nearly twenty years ago. Now we were all back together again as we celebrated a life that had touched so many.

Eventually, the cards stopped arriving in the mail. The phone calls were coming a little farther apart. Life was returning back to normal for everyone but me. I made daily trips to the cemetery. That dreadful finality of death that I had feared throughout my life was now my reality.

I read about the different stages of grief. I wondered how long it would take me to reach the last stage, *acceptance*. I wondered what exactly did *acceptance* mean? Did it mean I no longer felt any pain, sadness, loneliness? Did it mean time would simply erase all those emotions? There were times at the cemetery when I told God that if the sheer passage of time was going to make me forget Tom, then I didn't want to get over the pain of his loss. I didn't want to forget what the pain felt like.

I never quite felt the *denial* of his death. We had been on such a long journey with his illness for so many years. I had reconciled myself to the fact that given any unforeseen circumstances, he would probably die before me.

I certainly was *angry* about the way he died. What did chemotherapy have to do with a lung transplant? I fully expected his death to be associated with either complications related to the new lung or perhaps an infection in the remaining diseased lung. I never thought he would die of a raging infection caused by a low white blood cell count from chemotherapy treatments. And he only needed chemo because his new lung had a virus that had to be controlled by a powerful drug that had cancer as a possible side effect. The ironic part about it all was that his diseased lung that had not been replaced never had that virus.

I didn't feel any real *guilt* since I knew I had done everything I possibly could have done to help him live a longer and healthier life, although I did have some brief flashes of guilt for keeping him alive so long because of all he had endured. His words, "I don't want to leave you," had certainly urged me to do everything possible to keep him with me.

I read many articles about grief as I struggled with *depression and loneliness*. In one of them, it stated, "Sometimes all we really need is a hug." When I read that, I cried. It was indeed the loneliness that was slowly chipping away at my mental, emotional, and even my physical health. Along with an antidepressant, my doctor had prescribed medication to help me sleep.

I was living in a house crowded with silence. When I sat on the bench next to Tom's grave, I asked God over and over again why I felt so alone. I had so many people who loved me. Michelle and her family lived nearby, and I was welcome there any time. Andy had invited me to come and stay with him and his family. Why did I feel so alone when I truly wasn't alone at all? I knew God was always with me; I truly believed that. But it was the eye contact, the smile in the morning, the holding hands while walking, the talking and laughing together, the goodnight kiss—it was the human touch that was missing. Yes, sometimes all we need is a hug.

I bounced back and forth between these different stages of grief, all the while searching for a meaning. I couldn't accept Tom's death, and I felt as though I would never understand it.

Once I had survived the initial shock of grief, it became a much stealthier adversary. I never knew when a jolt of sadness was going to happen. While walking through the pharmacy department in a local grocery store, I glanced at a shelf and saw the eye drops Tom had taken for his macular degeneration, an eye disease that had progressed during his illness. I stood there and stared at the bottle for a minute, left the grocery cart right where it was, and went out to the car, only to feel my world fall apart all over again.

I knew Tom would not want me to be so sad, so lonely. One evening at home, I wrote a letter *to me from* Tom. I imagined what Tom would say to me if he could. I wrote about how he was free of pain. He was no longer suffering from all the complications and illnesses. He was at peace, and he wanted me to be happy too, to remember the love we shared, to not cry because he was gone but to be happy because we had had so many precious years together.

Writing that letter, like many other things, helped comfort me for a while, but I never knew how long it would last or what was going to trigger another wave of grief. Like the eye drops, it could be a song (especially "Unchained Melody"), a picture, the smell of his favorite food. There were so many things that caused that wave to come crashing down.

The flag flying in our backyard was a daily reminder of Tom's patriotism. I watched it blowing in the breeze and tried to understand how that patriotism had run so deeply in his soul even though his country had abandoned him when he returned home from the war. The repeated denials from the VA definitely contributed to that feeling of abandonment. We had received yet another denial from that organization several months before he died, but I kept my promise to him to work with Widener Law School and petition the VA for the 100 percent disability pension that he deserved.

I contacted the law school, and I made an appointment to meet with two research students to discuss Tom's case. The students were very kind and receptive to continuing research into the appeal process. When I left the meeting, I felt the usual frustration over the bureaucracy, but I was somewhat encouraged by the energy and enthusiasm the students had shown.

When I got home from that appointment, I had a voicemail from Linda, the woman from church who had sent so many cards and notes during Tom's illness. When I called her back, she offered to listen if I ever needed to talk to someone. That phone conversation lasted for over an hour and ended with Linda's inviting me to join her weekly Bible-study group that met at her home. Although I knew all the women in the group, I was hesitant to join. I wasn't sure where God was in my life just then.

A couple of weeks later, she called again to ask if I was ready to join, and I decided to give it a try. I needed to be around people. I fought back tears as best I could during the first lesson. I eventually broke down and cried uncontrollably, and these caring women cried with me. I was surrounded by loving people who hugged me tightly. Maybe God was showing me that I wasn't really alone after all. Maybe I would still feel some hugs.

When I got home from Bible study, I cried more. I cried for days. I think I cried more in the first month after Tom died than I did during the five years after his transplant. But now I had time to cry. My days were no longer filled with the endless caregiving tasks. It was the hollowest feeling I had ever felt in my life. It was as if my heart had been completely removed from my body, and I had no capacity to feel anything but emptiness. On some days, I was even unable to pray…and I hoped my tears were letting God know that I just couldn't talk.

A few weeks after Tom's death, I opened the weekly prayer request email from our church. There was a request for prayers for a woman, Wilma, who was facing some personal challenges. I had no idea what those challenges were, but I thought they couldn't be any worse than mine.

I didn't know who Wilma was, so I called Pastor Mary to get some more information. She told me that if I could help Wilma, it would be the answer to her prayers! I called the church office to get Wilma's phone number, and I called her the next day.

When Wilma answered the phone, she sounded as though she had been crying. I introduced myself and asked her if there was anything I could do to help. When she cried some more, I asked if I could come and meet her. She agreed and said I could meet her in front of the church, where she would be in her car.

I drove to the church and saw a black lady sitting alone in a car, but I had no idea if that was Wilma or not. As I walked toward the car, the passenger side window rolled down, and the woman looked my way. She had a kind-looking face, and I guessed she was probably in her late fifties or early sixties. I introduced myself, and she invited me to get in.

We talked for hours. She had worked at a customer service job for a local company for eighteen years, but the company had downsized several months ago, and she was let go. She was divorced, lived in a small apartment, and had been raising her eighteen-year-old grandson since he was two years old. She had no pension and had used her savings to pay rent and living expenses for them. She was now on the verge of eviction.

I didn't know what to say. She had graduated from Ohio State University; she had even been on the university debate team. I thought, *How could this happen?*

I asked her how I could help, and she said she would appreciate it if I could buy a few groceries for them.

Suddenly, my world was consumed with helping Wilma, or should I say Wilma's world was consumed with helping me? We met every day for several days and talked for hours. I told her all about Tom, and she cried with me. She told me about her military life with her husband and their subsequent divorce. She told me about the death of her thirty-two-year-old son, and I felt her pain deep in my heart. Once again, I felt God's presence. I needed her as much as she needed me, but then God had known that long before Wilma and I ever met.

After a few days went by without hearing from her, I was getting worried. Finally, she answered my call and explained that she had run out of minutes on her phone. She had to wait until her alimony check arrived before she could get more time added on. Her grandson had moved out, and she had been evicted from the apartment. She was living in her car.

When I went to meet her, she had a few bins filled with her belongings in the back seat, and some food items were on the front seat. The first thing we needed to do was to get her into a hotel room until we could decide what to do next. There were a few hotels in town that offered discounts for anyone coming in with a recommendation from the church. I called Pastor Mary, and she was able to help as we moved Wilma from one hotel to another for the next several weeks.

While helping Wilma, I made it a point to go to the weekly Bible-study meetings at Linda's home. She always had a thoughtful lesson prepared, and our discussions helped to extinguish that flame of anger that I had been harboring over Tom's death. Kathy and Mary Lou, the two nurses who had always paid so much attention to Tom at church, were part of this group. Their obvious love and concern for me were very comforting. We all discussed our own individual struggles in life, and their stories helped me to see how their trust in God had given them strength. I admired their courage. Through the love of this group, I saw that God had placed a healing opportunity in front of me.

I sometimes stayed after the lesson, and Linda and I talked more about its message. Regardless of what the lesson had involved, our conversation always led back to Tom. She was genuinely interested in our life together, and she listened intently to whatever I said. She somehow knew that I needed someone to be fully present to the magnitude of my loss without trying to point out a silver lining. She taught me better listening skills simply by truly listening to me. She lovingly accepted silence over conversation. She didn't try to talk me out of my grief. She allowed me to relive the unbearable. She allowed me to flounder in self-pity. And then she lovingly reminded me that our faith is like a seed; we water it with our tears, fertilize it with our pain, and then let the healing love of God shine upon us.

I thought back to the earlier times when Linda had called and wanted us to meet for lunch. I had been too consumed with Tom then, and I had kept saying, "Maybe another day." I thanked God for her patience.

Terri and Linda both wanted to know more about Wilma. They were concerned about her and began to help me look for a more permanent place for her to live. Terri was not feeling well again, but she scanned the newspapers and then let me know about places I should go visit.

Wilma couldn't afford much rent. When I went to visit the apartments that were in her price range, I usually turned around and left because they were either in terrible shape or in a dangerous neighborhood. I usually expressed my frustration to Wilma, but she remained hopeful. I was in awe of her cheerful attitude. She was homeless and constantly moving from one hotel to another with only a few belongings, but she never lost her sense of humor. We often talked about how we felt the hand of God, and we forged ahead one day at a time.

As the holidays approached, the tide of my grief kept swelling. Since Thanksgiving Day was also Tom's birthday, I decided to fly to Oregon and spend the holiday with Andy and his family. After Thanksgiving dinner, we each wrote a birthday note to Papa Tom and taped it to a balloon, then we released the balloons all at once and watched them float toward heaven.

The little grandkids went to their room and located *The Night Before Christmas*. It was one of those books that recorded your voices while reading the story. Tom and I had recorded it for them the previous year. When I heard his voice, my heart stopped. I couldn't cry in front of those happy little faces; instead, we huddled together and listened to Papa Tom talk about Santa and all his reindeer.

The trip to Andy's had been a helpful diversion from the loneliness at home. The only problem was that I had to return home. As I wheeled my suitcase in through the back door, the silence slapped me in the face. When I yelled, "Honey, I'm home," no one answered.

Life had always been busy, especially during the ten years that I had been a single mother. Andy and Michelle were good kids, but they engaged in typical sibling teasing and shouting matches, not to mention the challenges during those adolescent years! I had often thought, over those chaotic years, how pleasant it would be to have nothing to do, how peaceful it would be to simply sit and listen to silence. I never imagined silence could be so painful.

The trip to Andy's had helped get me through that first Thanksgiving holiday. Now I was facing Christmas. I had always enjoyed decorating our home. Tom would string white lights on the shrubs by the front porch. He wrapped the two white columns on either side in greenery and then hung a large red ribbon from the top of each one. I put candles in all the windows and set out various decorations of angels, Santa Claus, and winter scenes. After we had decorated the tree, we played Christmas carols and just enjoyed the joyful holiday atmosphere. We always went to the Christmas Eve service at church. After opening gifts on Christmas morning, we would take presents to Michelle and her family, and then stay for dinner.

THE AFTERMATH

This year was different. I didn't get a Christmas tree, and I didn't put up any decorations. I put a single candle in our bedroom window.

Michelle wanted me to stay with her and her family on Christmas Eve and then spend the next day with them—or as many days as I wanted to stay. I knew I wouldn't be very good company for the kids, so I spent the afternoon of Christmas Eve day at Terri's home. She didn't decorate much these days either. We talked about how things had changed so much. For years, we had taken turns fixing holiday dinners, and our homes had been filled with aunts, uncles, cousins, friends, and plenty of laughter.

I checked in on Wilma late that afternoon, and she assured me she was doing okay. She asked me to go to church with her for the Christmas Eve service, but I couldn't bring myself to go. I knew how much I would miss sitting next to Tom, feeling his arm gently resting on the pew behind me. I knew I would cry through the hymns and try not to sniffle through the prayers. I wasn't ready for well-meaning friends to express their sorrow again.

Christmas morning was heartbreaking. I didn't even want to get out of bed, but I had promised Michelle that I would be at her home for dinner. It was good to be around the little grandkids and watch their excitement as they showed me what Santa had brought them.

It was hard to accept that family holidays and gatherings were going to be so different now. Tom's absence lingered. I got stalled in grief. It was heavy, like a tremendous weight crushing me, and it took away my energy. I argued with this new forever-changed reality. I was living an uninvited life, and I fought it as hard as I could.

I let several people at church know about Wilma's situation, and many were willing to help. As I continued to work with her, a woman from church asked if I was interested in becoming a deacon. This was an ordained position within the church that was dedicated to visiting the sick and needy. As part of the church's visitation ministry, deacons needed to be available for errands and other services as needed.

I asked for a few days to consider it because I knew I was not very strong emotionally. What if I had to visit someone who had recently lost a loved one? I was not confident about my ability to be a comfort to anyone.

A few days later, on a very stormy evening, I was in the kitchen, washing dishes. Suddenly, I felt a tingling sensation throughout my entire body. Initially, I thought I was having a heart attack, so I sat down and tried to catch my breath. As the tingling became more intense, I was surprisingly no longer afraid. I knew this was a holy experience, and God was giving me a message. The kitchen was filled with a spirit that I could not describe. I soon found myself kneeling in the backyard in the pouring rain, looking upward, and thanking God for Tom. I felt Tom's kind and compassionate spirit all around me. I immediately realized that I truly did have a new direction in life. God was directing my attention *away* from myself and *toward* others.

I thought about all of the choices I had made during my life. Some were good; some were not so good. But I was convinced that I now had an important choice on my path that I had to make.

The next day, I called the woman from church, and I let her know that I was interested in becoming a deacon. I was still in complete awe of my experience the night before. The purpose for my remaining years was now crystal clear. I realized that my past experiences were actually gifts that God had given me so that I could help others!

My compassion for others had deepened because of all the tragic stories I had heard from women I served with in the air force. My empathy had deepened for those who were abused because of my first marriage and how I had struggled to leave it. My awareness of the suffering experienced by those who returned home from war was deepened because of how Tom had suffered. My understanding of conditions that lead to homelessness had deepened because of meeting Wilma and realizing how unforeseen life events can have sudden devastating effects. My ability to feel the deep pain of loss was because I had felt deep love and the agony that comes when it's gone.

I was to use these gifts to help others whenever and wherever possible. My purpose in life had nothing to do with *only what* had happened to me. It had everything to do with the meaning I gave to it and *how* I continued to move through life. I no longer searched for answers because the answers were already within me. This was a startling realization, and I was excited to get started.

I was vaguely aware of a Veterans Treatment Court in the area, so I decided to do some research on it. I learned it was a diversionary court that was offered to any eligible veteran who had been arrested and convicted of a crime. If all court-ordered programs were satisfactorily completed by the convicted veteran, it was possible for the charges to be dismissed by the court, thus giving the veteran another chance at having a law-abiding life. It was a remarkable concept and had been implemented in only a few states.

The court needed volunteer mentors, and a mentor had to be an honorably discharged veteran. Mentors were not permitted to give legal advice; instead, they were called upon to become a friend and confidant to the veterans in need. I immediately enrolled in the training, and I soon found myself helping veterans of all ages who were in trouble.

Each time I introduced myself to one of them, I told them that I had volunteered in memory of my husband, who had died as a result of the Vietnam War. This statement alone encouraged the veterans, male or female and regardless of age, to open up about their own experiences, particularly if they had been in combat.

If the veteran happened to be a Vietnam-era veteran, the stories came flooding out as if a dam had been breached in their hearts. They talked about the horrors of combat they had been engaged in, the senselessness of it all. They talked about watching their buddies die, about being evacuated in helicopters, about the monsoon rains and the blistering humidity of the jungles, about their anger at the protests back home, about how they had been treated as monsters when they arrived home, about how they struggled with fear, guilt, combat nightmares, and trying to escape it all through drugs and alcohol. They talked about feeling suicidal and the agony of buddies who had taken their own lives because they just couldn't cope. So many of these veterans were still suffering. Several had developed cancer because of their exposure to Agent Orange.

I knew Tom was watching and smiling as I worked with these veterans. It was not only their individual lives that had been so egregiously impacted; their addictions and diseases affected entire families for multiple generations. Each time I worked with a veteran, I thanked God for the opportunity to let my life's experiences have a positive impact on the life of another.

I had also heard about a program that was recognizing veterans who had died as a result of the Vietnam War. The memorial wall in Washington, DC, displayed the names of those who actually died during the war. This new program established a virtual wall and was attempting to identify those who had suffered and died of various service-connected health issues after the war but as a result of their deployment to Vietnam. After doing more research, I gathered the necessary documentation and submitted all the paperwork related to the circumstances of Tom's death.

As my days began to have meaning again, Terri's illness continued to progress, and she was scheduled for another round of chemotherapy. I took her to the treatments, and as I sat and watched the drug slowly drip into her body, my thoughts drifted back to when I had watched the same procedure performed on Tom. The harsh reality of it again frightened me.

I knew Terri was getting tired of it all because she never really felt good anymore. She was unable to travel. She had lost her appetite and no longer enjoyed going out for dinner. Tom's words echoed in my mind as I listened to her lament her situation. Since her mother's death, she had spent many hours home alone.

Our time together consisted mostly of long visits at her home. We always had plenty to talk about since we had been friends for over thirty-five years. She had been so helpful with my parental responsibilities of raising two children. She was always so willing to give me advice, but then she would laugh when I didn't take it. Ten years of operating our business together brought back constant laughter. Over the course of those years, Terri and I had talked many times about retiring one day. We knew that one day, all of the chaos would settle down. We had planned to buy two rocking chairs for each of our porches, so we always had a place to sit and laugh.

THE AFTERMATH

As the weeks went by, I continued to look for an apartment for Wilma, but I wasn't having much luck. Moving her from one hotel to another was not only tiring, it was expensive. We had learned which hotels gave the best offers, and we were always on the lookout for special weekly or monthly rates.

We also learned which hotels were repugnant. One morning, when I picked her up after the night at a hotel, I noticed her feet were swollen and covered with insect bites. She had spent the entire night sitting on a chair, trying to keep her feet off the floor to avoid getting bitten.

Once I got her checked into another hotel, I went to the pharmacy and bought a basin and some Epsom salts. Back in her room, I filled the basin with warm water and added the salt. Wilma sat on the edge of the bed, lowered her feet into the basin, and I washed and patted them dry. I felt so sorry for her that day. Washing her swollen feet was one of the most humbling experiences I had ever had.

After returning home later that evening, I found a letter from the Veterans Administration in the mailbox. I brought it inside and stood in the foyer, staring at it for several minutes. I asked Tom if I should open it. I wasn't sure how I would react when I read about yet another denial, and I felt the anger swell up inside me again.

When I opened it, I began reading the familiar "After further review," and my heart began to race. As I read on, I started shaking in disbelief. They had finally awarded Tom a 100 percent service-connected disability pension. I was infuriated. As I stood alone and held the letter that Tom had started looking for nearly thirteen years ago, I said out loud, "You bastards."

I took the letter and drove out to the cemetery to talk to Tom. And I cried. And I prayed. I thanked God that this cruel chapter was finally over. And once again I apologized to Tom from our "grateful nation."

Terri and Linda had both been appalled about the whole situation with the VA, but they were happy that it was finally over. I also let Tom's sisters Lois and MaryAnne know about the letter. They had both experienced Tom's torment from the war, and they had suffered with him throughout his years of alcoholism. He had spent time living with both of them during some of his homeless years.

The war had ended over forty years ago, and now the government (the "grateful nation") had finally acknowledged Tom's sacrifice—two years after he was gone. I thought about all of the veterans who had died feeling abandoned by their country. It made my work with the Veterans Court even more important.

As I continued my service as a deacon at the church, my work with the court, spending time with Terri, and looking for apartments for Wilma, my friendship with Linda grew closer. We went out for lunch frequently and took a few day trips together. I had dinner at her home several times. Her husband, Jim, welcomed me and made me feel very comfortable. He was interested in talking to me and asked lots of questions as we had engaging conversations. We started getting together regularly to play board games.

Much to my surprise, one day, Linda and Jim invited me to go on vacation with them for a week in Las Vegas. Initially, I declined because I didn't want to be the "third wheel," but they insisted, and I finally agreed. We caught an early-morning flight out of Philadelphia, and we talked and laughed for hours until we landed. The next several days were filled with more laughter and good times as we walked around the city. We had delicious dinners at elegant restaurants. We saw extravagant shows and laughed until we cried. We took a day trip to Lake Havasu to see the London Bridge, which had been relocated there from England in 1968. The bridge connected pedestrians, motorists, and cyclists on *mainland* Lake Havasu City to an island with shops, restaurants, and hotels. This had been one of Tom's favorite places when we had taken our cross-country trip years ago. I thought that was especially kind of them to take me back there.

On the flight home, my thoughts turned to Tom…and to God. I had convinced myself that I could not be happy again, but I was wrong. My friendship with Linda evolved into a deep, spiritual relationship. Although we had plenty of silly fun no matter what we did, our connection was on a much-different level than I had ever experienced with anyone else. When I told her about the holy experience in my kitchen that evening, she was not the least bit surprised. Her faith had actually deepened my faith. I had faith in a loving God, a God who was always with me even on days when I wasn't aware of it, a God who always knew when I needed help. Linda believed in a loving God too, but she also believed in a healing God, a God who knows your heart and doesn't want it to hurt, a God who whispers your name and breathes a little more strength into your body when you don't think you can go on.

Wilma and I often talked about the deep faith discussions that Linda and I had. This usually resulted in a reflective conversation between us as we talked about how important it was to trust God even when his timing doesn't make any sense to us. During Wilma's months of homelessness, her trust in God never wavered.

I eventually found an apartment for her. It was small and clean, and it was on a street only two blocks away from my home. It was perfect! When she had been evicted about a year before, we had moved her furniture to a storage facility in town. Once she signed the lease for her new apartment, several men from church helped to move the furniture in and get her established.

It seemed appropriate to have a housewarming party for her at my home. As she sat in the living room surrounded by a couple of dozen caring women, her face was radiant. I sat back and happily watched her open plenty of gifts. She got dishes, pans, a coffeepot, glasses, silverware, candles, grocery store gift certificates, various knickknacks, and even some household cleaning supplies. I smiled as I listened to the laughter throughout the house once again. Wilma and I had been complete strangers just a year ago. We had laughed and cried and prayed together during some very difficult days and nights. She had joined the church and had made many new friends. I marveled at the scene before my eyes, and I knew God was smiling too.

I had read somewhere that "if you don't have a problem, that's your problem." How true that is! God opens some doors very quietly. I had had no idea what my initial phone call to Wilma would uncover. When I had witnessed her homelessness and experienced her seemingly hopeless situation, I knew God was teaching me a lesson. Wilma's problem had become my problem. When Wilma had observed my search for a new identity, my wandering through seemingly hopeless days, my problem had become Wilma's problem. I watched Wilma's dignity grow. She watched my capacity to love expand.

After Tom had died, I needed to feel needed. I had now learned that the best way for me to feel needed was to make someone else feel needed. The best way to feel loved was to make someone else feel loved. The best way to cure loneliness was to visit a lonely person.

Throughout all of these months, Terri was really struggling with her illness, and she lost her optimistic outlook. One day, she told me that she wasn't sure we would be sitting in those rocking chairs together as we had always talked about. That was a crushing thought.

My time with her was always focused on being positive, encouraging, and remembering the good times we had had. That laughter always helped get her through those days. It helped me too, but I wish we would have cried together.

*****

Hovering over this part of my virtual tour brought back feelings of intense loneliness that I was not prepared for. Initially, I focused on the pain of my loss, bouncing around all the stages of grief, and not finding any meaning.

I had spent countless hours sitting on a bench by Tom's grave; it was a lonely place. As I sat there, I watched other grieving people come and go. Some people brought lawn chairs and stayed for hours, reading a book. Others came and stood in complete silence with their heads bowed and hands folded in prayer. Once a woman came and lay down on a grave and sobbed. Each time, I wondered whom they had lost and what their life had been like. Sometimes I was the only person there, bundled up in a heavy coat and sitting in the cold wind or wearing shorts and T-shirt and sweltering in the summer heat.

One day, looking out across the cemetery, I realized that deep grief is caused by deep love. And how fortunate are those of us who

THE AFTERMATH

have felt such deep love. I never looked at those grieving visitors the same way after that.

And then God had sent me a strong message. As a deacon at my church and a volunteer mentor at the Veterans Court, I became useful again. And I thought about Wilma. What a void she had filled in my life. As I helped her get back on her feet, she had exposed me to an unfamiliar world of hardship, homelessness, and hope.

Terri was still fighting her illness, but we managed to always laugh at our past together, even making new memories as I pushed her through the mall in her wheelchair so she could buy "skinny clothes."

I realized that not only did I have the gift of treasured memories that comforted me; I discovered there were many people who needed my help. It felt like both were halves of a healing whole.

*****

Reflections

1. Time is a great healer, but it never quite blunts the loneliness that loss brings. Living the unlivable and bearing the unbearable are part of the grieving process. Helping others will not only occupy our time, it may help us see our loss and the world in a brighter light. Have you found any possibilities through a loss or difficult experience? How have you used them to help others?

   _____
   _____
   _____
   _____

2. Tears are a form of prayer when we are unable to speak or rationalize our thoughts. They can be tears of joy or gratitude, or they can be tears caused by deep grief or sorrow. Do you think tears make you vulnerable? When have you cried tears that helped to heal you?

   _____
   _____
   _____
   _____

3. What we understand about ourselves and life is demonstrated by the way we live. Every act is an act of self-definition. Is your behavior true to who you really are?

   _____
   _____
   _____
   _____

CHAPTER 13

Cumulative Grief

Wilma was doing well in her new apartment. It was gratifying to see her become more stable and independent. I visited her often and always picked her up for church on Sunday mornings.

Even though I had started to find a purpose in my life again, grief moved in and out of my days like waves crashing on the beach and then receding back into the ocean. It lurked just beneath the surface, waiting for an opportunity to lash out and drown me in a sea of emotions. At times, I felt like I was in a dark wilderness, isolated and alone and not really caring if I found my way out. Then there were days when I felt as though my strength and independence were coming back, only to be replaced with that overpowering sense of loss again.

At this most vulnerable time in my life, I found myself relying on Linda for emotional support. I was aware of that need, and I didn't like it. She continued to gently probe, asking questions and praying with me. She also talked about her life and some of the struggles she had faced. I was pleased, not only because our friendship had deepened but also because the focus of the discussion was not on me. I wanted to offer her the same degree of comfort that she had given me.

One week, Linda asked me to be in charge of her Bible-study lesson. That meant I had to read, research, plan, and get organized for the meeting. I felt completely unqualified to be tasked with such a responsibility, so I declined. Even though she disagreed with me and thought that I was capable, she respected my position. A few weeks later, she said she didn't feel well, and she asked me again if I would fill in for her. Of course, I wanted to help, so I prepared the lesson and facilitated the meeting. To my surprise, the lesson went well, and I actually enjoyed it. Instead of just showing up and listening, the lesson preparation made me think more about the content. As I focused more on the message, I felt more at peace and actually closer to God. I often wondered if Linda hadn't subtly maneuvered me into doing that lesson!

Many times, I discussed the Bible lessons with Terri. We had a very lively discussion on her next trip to the oncologist in Philadelphia; however, the ride home was silent. Her health had not improved much since the last round of chemotherapy, and the doctor had suggested going through more treatments. He told us about a new type of chemo he was using on patients and with encouraging results. Terri had previously been through a volunteer trial program for a new drug, but she had shown no improvement. She felt she had had enough, and she told the doctor she was no longer interested in *any* treatment. After a brief discussion, it was obvious she wasn't going to change her mind. This was news to me as well as the doctor. He said he would get in touch with the hospice organization near her home and make arrangements for palliative care.

Our ride home was quiet for a long time, mostly because I was choking back tears. Terri finally talked about how she was "sick of being sick." Her quality of life had certainly deteriorated, and I understood what she was saying. She told me that unlike with Tom, it was not my responsibility to keep her alive. It was a sobering remark. Then as always, she put her positive foot forward and tried to lighten up the rest of the ride home.

When I got back home, there was a letter notifying me that Tom had been accepted for recognition by the organization honoring veterans who had died as a result of the Vietnam War. I was invited to participate in the memorial service in Washington, DC, in a few months. I immediately started organizing the trip to ensure that all my family and Tom's family could attend. I also reserved hotel rooms for Terri and one for Linda and Jim. It was going to be quite a celebration!

Within a week or two, a hospice nurse arrived at Terri's home for the initial consultation. I was unable to be there, but she called that evening to tell me about it. The nurse was a man, and she liked his positive attitude and caring manner. The tone of her voice was not only optimistic, but it was cheerful. I was anxious to meet this guy!

The nurse's name was Pat, and he was required to visit Terri every two weeks. I made sure I was there the next time he arrived, and I saw that he did indeed have a very caring manner and positive attitude. He took a lot of time to explain his role in her care. They joked and laughed together, and Terri definitely had a better frame of mind than she had had in quite a while. I smiled all the way home.

Linda was also happy to hear the good news about Terri's improved attitude. We talked, as we had so many times, about the ways in which God presents people when we seem to need them the most. Even though he was with Terri because of her failing health, Pat's presence took her mind off of her disease, and she felt energized about life again.

As I began to worry a little less about Terri, I decided to go to a family function in New Jersey with Jim and Linda. We went to a Memorial Day barbecue at the home of their daughter April and her family. April had the same silly sense of humor as her mother, so there was a lot of laughter, and we got along very well.

About a week later, Linda called and asked if I would go to the pharmacy and pick up a prescription for her. She had not been feeling well for a few days with a cold and a slight fever. A painful earache had developed overnight, so she had seen the doctor that morning and was given prescriptions for an antibiotic and pain medication. Jim was working, and she needed the medicine as soon as possible.

When I took the medications to her, I could tell she was in a lot of pain. We visited until she needed to lie down for a while. When Jim got home, he called and thanked me for bringing the medicine and said Linda was sleeping. Later that evening, she called and said her ear still hurt, but she was hopeful it would be better by morning.

We expressed our concern for each other and said the usual "night, night—love you."

The next afternoon, Jim called me from the emergency room at the local hospital. Linda's pain was worse. In addition to an earache, she had pain throughout her head. I went immediately to the emergency room and waited with Jim for hours while the doctor came in and out, and a few tests were performed. Finally, the doctor said there was nothing they could pinpoint that might be causing such pain, so they admitted her for the night for observation.

Late in the evening, I told Jim to go home and rest since he had been there most of the day. I told him I would stay with her through the night and then go home in the morning when he came back.

It was a long night, and I sat by her bed the entire time. The nurse came in a few times to check on her, and a lab technician came to draw some blood. I was at a total loss about what could cause such pain. Linda was sleeping soundly, but I was frightened. I earnestly prayed that the morning would bring good news.

When Jim and April arrived in the morning, Linda was still sleeping. Since I had been up all night, I went home to get some rest and told them to call me if anything changed. When I woke up a few hours later, I called Jim to see if there was any news, and he was quite upset. Linda was awake, in terrible pain, and was hallucinating. The doctors could not determine what was causing such pain, so they were attempting to get a room for her at the University of Pennsylvania Hospital in Philadelphia. After several frustrating and agonizing hours, a room became available, and the doctor scheduled an ambulance to take her there.

I went home, packed an overnight bag, and drove to the hospital to wait for them. By the time the ambulance arrived, Linda was in respiratory distress, and she was put on a ventilator. The doctor met with all of us, and he was not very optimistic about treatment. He said they first had to get her stabilized and breathing on her own before any significant tests could be done.

Both of Linda's children and their spouses were there, and the next several days were grueling for everyone as we watched and waited. We met with a team of doctors each day. They all agreed that Linda needed to be off the ventilator before an MRI of her brain could be performed. In the meantime, they conducted numerous tests and blood work to rule out potential causes of her pain. In an attempt to help her breathe on her own, she spent two days lying on her stomach to take the pressure off her lungs.

Her children adjusted their work schedules so they could be there as much as possible. Jim and I sat in her room, slept in the chairs, and talked for hours. When I wasn't sitting in Linda's room, I wandered around the halls of the hospital, the same halls I had wandered when Terri was there for her stem cell transplant six years before. I located the same hospital chapel, and I sat for hours and prayed. I couldn't believe this was happening, and those dreaded *why* questions were again part of my prayers.

After a few days, there was a ray of hope when Linda began to breathe just a little better on her own, but it was not enough to remove the ventilator. On a morning when I had run my finger along the bottom of her foot, it wiggled. We were all thrilled that she was finally starting to wake up. As it turned out, that wiggle was an involuntary action. She was still only showing the slightest sign of breathing on her own, and the doctors were concerned. With the family's permission, they decided to go ahead with an MRI of her brain.

Jim and I were sitting in her room when the doctor came in and told us what we had all feared for days. Linda had meningitis of the brain, and she was not going to wake up. The news was crushing, and shock set in. April and her husband arrived just after the doctor left the room. One look at her dad, and she knew what had happened. She screamed, "I hate you, God!"

As they hugged and cried, I left the room and went to the small chapel downstairs. I was in the chapel, but I didn't want to talk to God. I didn't pray for anything. Hours later, I packed my bag and drove home. Our family gathering for Tom's ceremony in Washington, DC, was scheduled for the next day.

My body ached. My mind was jumbled with thoughts that ranged from a deep, numbing sadness for having to leave Linda to gratification and pride for Tom's being recognized at the upcoming veterans' ceremony. I felt my soul being ripped apart by such conflicting emotions. I felt as though I was in and out of reality.

The next day, Terri rode to Washington, DC, with me, and we picked up Lois and MaryAnne at the airport. Andy and his family arrived from Oregon, and Michelle and her family came a little later. I stayed in the room reserved for Jim and Linda. Terri completely understood that I wanted to be alone.

We all gathered at the hotel restaurant for dinner that night. The grandchildren were lively and thoroughly enjoyed the attention from the adults. Since Andy lived so far away, the kids seldom got to spend time together, so it was very special to see them playing together. I watched it all through a fog. I'm sure I was the last to fall asleep that night and the first to wake in the morning. I talked to Tom and told him how proud I was that he was finally being recognized for his sacrifice. Although I knew I should, I still didn't talk to God. I couldn't think of anything to say.

The ceremony was held outside, and hundreds of people were there to recognize their loved ones. We waited our turn and finally walked up on stage. I choked back tears as I read Tom's name, branch of service, and years of service in Vietnam. When I saw all the little grandchildren dressed in red, white, and blue, I knew Tom was bursting with pride.

After saying all our goodbyes, Terri and I started the trip back home. She knew how I had struggled over the past two days, but she talked about all the highlights of the program and how enjoyable the kids had been. Just then, my phone rang. It was Jim calling from the hospital. Linda was gone. We drove home in silence. There were simply no words.

The church was full of friends and family for Linda's funeral. Pastor Mary had retired and moved out of state, and I thought that was exceptionally sad because Linda had admired her so much. She had made Tom's memorial service very special, and I felt her absence was yet another loss.

When I stood up during the service to say a few words, I saw Terri sitting near the back of the church. I instantly felt even more grateful for her presence in my life.

CUMULATIVE GRIEF

In the weeks following Linda's death, I tried desperately to understand what had happened. Although I never understood why Tom had to suffer so much, I knew how sick he was, and I knew what the future ultimately held. Because Linda had died so suddenly and unexpectedly, it called for a different kind of coping, one blanketed by shock. There had been no time to prepare for this change that shattered my daily life. My heart was broken, and my bones ached day and night. Sometimes, it was hard to just breathe.

In the days ahead, Jim and I stayed in touch and began spending more time together since each of us had now lost our soulmate. We could cry without needing to explain why. We could sit in silence without feeling uncomfortable. We each knew the depth of the loss. We were each filled with love, but there was no longer any place for it to go.

Terri and I talked every day. I would have visited her more often, but I hated to interrupt the good time she was having with Pat, her hospice nurse. He had brought a lot of laughter into her life, and that is what she needed the most. Besides, laughter was something that was difficult for me to find.

April was devastated by her mother's death, and I tried to send her encouraging text messages each morning and evening. I was very careful to not cross over any boundaries where she might think I was trying to take her mother's place. I told her I was very sensitive to that concern, and I asked her to let me know if she ever felt that was happening.

Many times, when I visited Linda at the cemetery, I explained this same worry to her, and I asked her for guidance. We had agreed that whichever one of us died first, the one remaining would help take care of either April or Michelle.

As the holidays approached, I thought about all the times that Michelle and I had traveled to New York City. Sometimes it was for the day, and sometimes we stayed overnight at a hotel in Times Square. Our first trip was when she was about nine years old, and then we continued to travel there every year for fifteen years. We always saw a Broadway play and then walked around and marveled at the Christmas decorations in the store windows. It was wonderful "girl time" together, and we made such special memories. Our trips ended when the little grandbabies were born, and life was too busy for such frivolous trips!

Remembering those special times, I asked April if she would like to take the train to New York City and spend the day looking at the Christmas decorations. I was thrilled when she said she would like to go, and I hoped it would help relieve some of the deep pain she felt from missing her mother during the holiday season.

Once the train arrived in New York City, we went to St. Patrick's Cathedral to light a candle for Tom and one for her mother. After leaving the church, we started walking down a crowded Fifth Avenue when suddenly, a small piece of yellow paper floated down in front of April. "Did you see that!?" she shouted with wide eyes.

"See what?" I asked.

With a look of disbelief, she said, "That piece of paper had my mom's name on it!"

We looked down at the ground and found the paper upside-down on the sidewalk. April picked it up and turned it over. In all capital letters, "LINDA" was written on it. I looked at April, and then I looked straight up and saw nothing but skyscrapers and a blue sky.

Here in the midst of the holiday hustle and bustle on Fifth Avenue, this small piece of yellow paper had come floating down from *somewhere* and landed at our feet. Linda's favorite color was yellow; it was truly miraculous. We both knew instantly that Linda was with us as we shared this special day, and I knew she approved of our trip because she had just given me the sign that I needed.

After the holidays, I decided to resume the weekly Bible-study meetings with the women from church. I knew it was going to be a daunting task, but I also knew it was what Linda wanted me to do. They were such a caring group of women, and I needed to be with them. I also needed God back in my life. Since I wanted to invite someone else to join our group, I thought of Deb. I had talked to her briefly a few times at church, and although I didn't know her very well, I remembered something special about her. When I was in the hospital chapel, feeling very alone and praying for Linda to wake up, a text message from Deb suddenly appeared on my phone.

She wanted me to know that she was thinking of me and praying for both Linda and me. That message touched my heart. I have since wondered if it hadn't been a gentle nudge from God to let me know, once again, that I was not going to be alone.

The weeks and months went by, and Jim and I settled into a routine of frequent dinners together. The companionship was something we both needed. I was grateful that it had blossomed into a best-buddy relationship. The tears still fell freely. The memories we shared brought both pain and joy.

I continued to take Terri out for long rides in the countryside just as I had done with Tom. Her disease had taken a serious downward turn, and she had lost more weight. I went to her house every day to fix a meal, but she couldn't keep anything down. Pat and another hospice nurse came almost daily to check on her. Everyone was very worried.

One day, when Terri was feeling especially bad, she wanted us to decide on a *sign* that she could give me once she was gone. She knew how comforting heavenly signs were for me. Regrettably, I refused to discuss such a topic because I simply didn't want to face what she was telling me.

A few days later, the hospice nurse called and told me Terri's condition was very grave. When I arrived at her house, the nurse said she would probably die within twenty-four to forty-eight hours. When she left, I went back to Terri's bedroom. She was on oxygen, sleeping, and having great difficulty breathing.

As she gasped for air, I sat next to her bed and held her hand. I started to talk about all the good times we had shared over the years, and I thanked her for her friendship. I had talked to her about these things after her stem cell transplant so many years ago because it was good *medicine* and made us both laugh. Now I began saying the same things, only this time, it was for a very different reason. It was part of my final goodbye.

I thanked her for helping me raise Andy and Michelle during those first years after my divorce. She had given me the courage to leave the marriage...and so much more.

I reminded her of the time we got caught in a thunderstorm at a concert. We were soaking wet and miserable as we sat on the long bus ride home, and we had laughed about it for years.

I talked about painting that fence and how much we had laughed, even drenched in turpentine, while cleaning up.

I talked about all the characters we had met during our ten years in business.

- Remember the client who was an insurance agent and had a strange rubber mask of a chicken hanging on the coatrack in his office? What was that all about? Oh, how we laughed when we finally finished our meeting with him and went outside.
- Remember the client who was literally frightened of her computer, and we had to constantly reassure her that she wasn't going to break it?
- Remember the client who always looked so sad and never wore a shirt that wasn't wrinkled? We felt so sorry for him that we almost wrote his system for free!
- Remember how you quit your job without telling me? I was shocked, and you just laughed!
- Remember how thrilled we felt when we first bought our own homes? You bought the pretty Victorian home that you had always wanted, and I ended up living on the street that I had always dreamed of.
- Remember how you loved to give advice that I never took?
- Remember all the nights out dancing and the time I slipped on the dance floor and twisted my ankle? When we left the hospital emergency room with a splint and crutches, I looked like I had a broken leg, and you couldn't stop laughing!
- Remember the endless hours we used to talk on the phone and laugh about the silliest things?

The more I talked, the calmer her breathing became. Although she never woke up, I was sure she heard me. I hoped she couldn't hear how my voice was quivering. As I was thanking her one more time for blessing my life in so many ways, she took her last breath.

Terri was gone. I had just reminded her of our thirty-five years of friendship, a friendship that had sustained both of us through good times and bad times. I thought about those two rocking chairs we had intended to sit on and reminisce about the decades we spent together.

I sat next to her for a long time and held her hand. I felt God's presence in her room, and it was the most sacred moment of my life. I realized that I had peacefully helped my dearest friend move through the gates of heaven.

I felt warm tears fill my eyes, but there was also a tender smile on my face, and I went home.

*****

As I hovered over these years, I thought about how the bond that links your true family together is not always one of blood but one of respect and joy in sharing each other's life. I thought about how much I missed Terri and Linda and how I had struggled to live with the huge gaping holes of their absence.

I thought about how cruel loss can be. On those days when you think you're finally getting past the pain, all of a sudden, you see or hear something, and that memory douses the day with sadness.

As with Tom's death, the *why* questions came up again. But now, there were new questions. Whom do I have left in my life? Whom do I call when I hear a funny story? Whom do I send the cute picture of my grandchildren to? Where do I go to just sit and visit the day away?

And finally, I thought about how grief needs to be shared if it is to eventually morph into a degree of joy. I now understood that I suffered from unresolved cumulative grief. Although I had found purpose for my life, I was still grieving for Tom when Linda died. And less than a year later, I had to say goodbye to Terri.

Although we all have to chart our own course of recovery through grief, I had continued to fight it. I had let grief define me as a person. I had been resisting God's invitation to accept my losses. And because I resisted, it persisted.

*****

Reflections

1. Grief is deeply personal. Some days we feel strong enough to cope with intense feelings; other days we feel like giving up. If you have experienced multiple losses—whether the loss of a loved one, a job, a relationship, a sense of independence or mobility—have you processed each one separately, or have you let them overwhelm you? Please explain.

   _____
   _____
   _____
   _____

2. Have you been affected by the legacy left behind from the death of a loved one, either the legacy of their life or the legacy of your time with them? How has it impacted how you are living your life now?

   _____
   _____
   _____
   _____

3. Relationships with friends and family members are unique to each of us. How fulfilling and supportive are your relationships with each? Is there anything you can do to make them more meaningful?

   _____
   _____
   _____
   _____

CHAPTER 14

Don't Ask Why

The days and weeks went by, and I found myself going through the motions and sometimes not even knowing what day it was. I buried myself in my volunteer duties, but I faced long, empty evenings and weekends. Jim and I kept in touch and even did some traveling. I kept the weekly Bible-study sessions going. But the void that opened when Tom died had now expanded with the absence of both Linda and Terri.

Terri had been cremated, and her sister kept the urn. This was very upsetting because I didn't have that physical place to be alone with her, and I missed her terribly. I made regular trips to the cemetery where Tom was buried and another one several miles away where Linda was buried. It always brought me comfort to sit and talk to them. I needed a sense of connection. I needed to reflect on our memories. I needed to talk about what I was doing and how I was trying to move forward.

When I was growing up, thoughts of dying were scary, and there were lots of reminders. There were sayings like "end of the line," "final curtain call," and "final judgment." Someone who was badly mistaken was "dead wrong." What about the spirit that comes for your soul, the Grim Reaper? There were "dead-end streets" that supposedly went nowhere although oftentimes dead-end streets are simply a place to turn around.

During young adulthood, I chose not to think much about death. During the early years of my first marriage, with the fear and challenges of living in an abusive marriage, small children, and a career, I had been too busy to give death much thought. With the death of my parents and grandparents, deep sadness had set in as I reflected back on the important and loving roles they had all played in my life. Death felt much more real. With each of those deaths, I felt as though a piece of my very being was lost forever.

Losing loved ones, saying that forever goodbye, was agonizing. After I lost Tom, Linda, and Terri, grief engulfed and overwhelmed me. I didn't want that new forever-changed reality. I know now that I fought accepting my losses, and as a result, I made life more difficult for myself.

My virtual tour clearly showed me that God had been teaching me, guiding me, providing for me, loving me, protecting me, and giving me opportunities to grow throughout my life. I learned that asking the question *why* is a desperate and useless endeavor, one we may never understand this side of heaven.

I used to ask, "Why did Tom have to suffer so much during his life?" I used to ask, "Why did Linda have to die so tragically and unexpectedly?" I used to ask, "Why did Terri have to get a rare blood disease and die at an early age?" I used to ask, "Why am I the only one left?"

Now I ask *what*. What can I do with the knowledge I've gained and the experiences I've lived as I've grieved? Surely these scars have been carved into my heart for a reason.

Why did Tom have to suffer so much during his life? I still don't know the answer to that question, but what I do know is that because of Tom, I am a better person. I am less selfish and more empathetic. I understand better the horrors associated with post-traumatic stress disorder in veterans, the complexities associated with transplant patients and medications, and the grueling responsibilities of caregiving.

So *what* can I do with this knowledge? Because of Tom, I now volunteer to help troubled veterans. Tom's sacrifices taught me to understand more deeply. His unconditional love taught me to be more accepting, more forgiving. His mature love taught me how to love with more compassion and respect.

Why did Linda have to die so tragically and unexpectedly? I still don't know the answer to that question either, but what I do know is that Linda also made me a better person. My faith and trust in God are deeper and more meaningful.

But *what* can I do with my faith? I continue to create weekly Bible-study lessons, and Linda's faith, through me, is deepening the faith of those in our study group. Now I try harder to always listen more intently to those who are speaking. I listen with my heart. Linda's genuine tenderness enabled me to love more openly.

Why did Terri have to get a rare blood disease and die at an early age? Here, too, I don't know the answer, but what I do know is that because of Terri, my life has also been enhanced. Terri taught me the influence of positive energy and the healing power of laughter. She taught me to seek strength and find hope in the most impossible situations.

But *what* can I do with those attributes? Terri's authentic love of life taught me there is hope in any situation, so I can be the kind of friend to others that Terri was for me. I can lead by example and encourage others to have hope, to find laughter, to remember the strength that is in them always.

The culmination of all my experiences guided me to the local hospice center where I am a volunteer chaplain. During my grief journey, I would have never dreamed I would have the strength to comfort the dying and their friends and families. My patient visits consist of sharing the love and the lessons I have lived, listening intently to their stories, and praying for those headed down a path I have already traveled.

Why am I the only one left? That is a question that I should have never asked because God has been with me every step of the way. It was God sending me those heavenly signs from lost loved ones. I was never truly alone.

Sometimes my prayers for understanding were no more than the moaning of my heart, but God heard every one of them. Prayer is a powerful way of embracing life. Prayer is a powerful way of finding a home in *any* outcome. Prayer is a powerful way of remembering that there may be reasons beyond reason.

The reality is that I will grieve forever. I will not get over these losses, but instead, I will continue to learn to live with them. I will heal and recreate myself around them. I will be whole again, but I will never be the same.

Grief transformed my life. I learned that on the other side of grief is joy, pure joy in having had people to love so deeply. Without a doubt, I felt true and nearly paralyzing pain when I lost them. I deeply mourned their loss, but I also ignored their happiness as they returned home to God.

I learned that suffering is optional. Certainly, it was my unconscious decision not to let go. I desperately struggled to hold on to their love, to their warm touch, to their laughter. By resisting the acceptance of my losses, my suffering persisted. It was not until I found meaning and could let go that the suffering went away. The sincere gratitude for having them in my life outweighed the horror of the losses.

Fully trusting in God transformed my life. God loves me and has the power to help me heal, but I needed to do my part also. I needed to stop focusing on my losses. Each life was indeed a gift. Each life enriched my own life, taught me important lessons. With the loss of each life, God had given me an opportunity to allow those lessons to become blessings to others.

I have looked back over the years through this virtual tour, and it has been remarkable to see precisely *how* God was always at work in my life. I discovered that blessings come during both good times and bad times. And although the blessings are sometimes difficult to recognize, we have the freedom to choose how to respond to each one. We can find hope, or we can find despair. Much like that dead-end street, we can see our loss as a place of no return, or we can humbly recognize it as a place to turn around and move forward again. It is our choice.

I continue to thank God for my Bible-study group. These women share personal stories that deepen our relationships. I find strength through them, and they help me to not only understand but also to appreciate differing viewpoints and perspectives.

I continue to thank God for Linda's family. They adopted me as part of their family. I became close friends with some of their friends. Jim and I remain *buddies*. April and I have a special bond that will always be nurtured through love for her mother.

I continue to thank God for Wilma, whom I lost during the writing of this book. Her death was tragically unnecessary due to a blundered medical procedure—again, something difficult to understand. The profound role that she played in my life still amazes me. She appeared because I had answered an email prayer request from our church. Not knowing her or what might lay ahead, it was God's perfect timing, and we each filled a void that neither of us could have envisioned.

I continue to thank God for new opportunities and for special people. Louise is someone who had attended the same church that Tom and I attended. Like Linda, she had also observed my losses from a distance and then, unexpectedly, called one afternoon. Because she reached out to me, we had numerous deep and meaningful conversations that explored our faith. Her presence in my life added another layer of comfort at just the right time. Again, I believe God guided her to me when I needed her most.

I continue to thank God for my siblings, and for the solid foundation that Mom and Dad had provided for us. Although we don't see each other as often as we once did, I take great comfort in knowing that we share a common bond steeped in deep love and respect.

I also lost my younger brother Mark while writing this book. He died of Lou Gehrig's disease only six months after his diagnosis. It was extremely painful to watch this disease rob him of all voluntary muscle movement. During his illness, we shared our thoughts about death, dying, and faith in God. The dreaded *why* question came up, but we both understood that some things are simply not to be understood. His faith was unshakeable. His courage was humbling.

I continue to thank God for my children and their families. Andy and Michelle had a turbulent early childhood, and they don't remember a lot of it, but through God's grace, their later years were peaceful, and they have the blessed capacity to love. I am so proud of who they have become. Cole, Chase, Jocelyn, Matty, and Gracie fill their grandmother's heart with an abundance of pride and joy.

The heavenly signs that I received from Dad, Tom, Linda, Terri, and other lost loved ones reassured me that I was not alone. The more open I was to believing in these signs, the more often they appeared. Pictures of that afterlife that I once feared softened.

The most important lesson that I learned from my journey through grief was that once I took my attention away from myself, I became more aware of the needs of others. I learned that my life is not about me; it is about all the lives that I can touch and how I can have a positive impact on them. I learned that my experiences, both good and bad, and the lessons learned from them were always intended to become blessings to others.

Death no longer scares me as it once did. I believe that death is simply a continuation of our soul into the afterlife. Even though we are placed in situations that we don't want and we suffer from pain we didn't create, we are here to fulfill our soul's agenda.

Once again, my purpose here has nothing to do with only the circumstances of my life. It has everything to do with how I respond to those situations, how I see them as opportunities and move forward, how I can touch the lives of others.

I learned that no matter how my life unfolds, with ease and grace or with pain and suffering, there is a higher power in control. I learned to trust what I don't understand.

*****

I hovered over the years of my life, and it reminded me of putting a puzzle together. At first, I dumped out all of the pieces. This was the pile of years that had gone by.

When I started sorting through them, I set the edge pieces aside. Those years were the easy years. They made the most sense, and they fit together nicely.

Then I grouped the pieces into similar colors and patterns. Those were the various stages of my life.

Then I started putting the puzzle together. This took time and patience!

Sometimes the pieces fit together easily. These were the years when times were good, and life was less complicated.

Other areas were a struggle, especially when the pieces all looked alike (a blue ocean or a dark sky). These were years when I struggled to understand what was happening in my life, the chaotic first marriage and the devastating deaths of loved ones.

I got frustrated at times because the pieces didn't fit right, and I just had to walk away. These were years where I chose to suffer. I was overwhelmed and stalled, unable to move forward.

Just as I thought a piece was missing, I looked under the table and found it on the floor. Those were the years when I truly turned to God and began to understand that my experiences (both good and bad) were actually helping me to grow.

I learned that my mind creates responses and solutions based upon the information that it has stored over the years. But although my body responds to what my mind creates, the true answers lie within my soul.

*****

Reflections

1. *Why* is the most useless question. *What* is the most fruitful question. Describe an experience in your life when asking, "What can I do about it?" helped you move forward.

   _____
   _____
   _____
   _____

2. How have you made your life more difficult by not accepting something you couldn't change? Please explain.

   _____
   _____
   _____
   _____

3. Sadness can be an indication of the depth of our feelings, of who we are as a person and spiritual being. Without sadness, we would not know happiness. Do you believe happiness will return as you allow your grief to move further away? Please explain.

   _____
   _____
   _____
   _____

CHAPTER 15

Signs, Gratitude, and Meaning

My virtual tour is over, and I have landed in reality, back to the realm of physical beings where life continues amid the cumulative and collective losses of so many. Death happens every day, sometimes unexpectedly, sometimes as a relief after much suffering. It is something that used to frighten me because the concept of *forever* was hard to comprehend. The thought of it would make my insides quiver. I wasn't sure what that afterlife looked like.

One day, as I was leaving the cemetery after I had spent some time praying by Tom's grave, I saw a woman sitting on the ground next to a gravestone at the back of the property. This was not an unusual sight as I had seen many people doing that during my visits, but this time, something felt different. I got in my car and watched her for a long time. I was trying to decide if I should interrupt her special time so that I could say a prayer with her. I drove around to the back of the cemetery, hoping that she would look up, and I could catch her eye. But she didn't. I finally decided to stop the car and get out and walk over. When I got near her, she looked up with tears streaming down her face. I leaned over and introduced myself, and I told her that I had been visiting my late husband. I asked her if she would like a prayer. She said yes, and when I asked her who she was grieving for, she said it was her dad. He had died three years before of cancer.

She talked for quite a while about what a good man he was and how much she missed him. She said she usually came here with her husband and children, but today, she wanted to come alone. There was a sadness in her voice that sounded far too familiar, and it was hard to choke back tears. When I said, "Let's pray," she turned slightly, looked me straight in the eyes, and took both of my hands. When I asked her what her name was, she said, "Terri."

Once again, I felt this as yet another heavenly sign that someone I loved was not far away. I felt as though Terri had sensed my loneliness and had used this young lady to let me know that she was near.

There was another time when I had visited Tom's grave and felt that he truly knew I was there. Once I left the cemetery, I turned on the car radio, and a man's voice said, "Thank you for coming." I was so shocked by that single sentence that I had to pull off to the side of the road to try and understand what had just happened. That was all the man said before regular station music started playing again. It was astounding!

I remembered another time when I had been visiting April. We were standing in her kitchen and talking about her mother. She took a few steps into the dining room to get something. All of a sudden, we heard Alexa say, "Night, night. Love you."

April came around the corner wide-eyed, looked at me, and asked, "What did you say?"

I looked at her wide-eyed, shrugged my shoulders, and said, "I didn't say anything!"

Her son was downstairs, and he came up to see who had said, "Night, night. Love you."

We were all stunned. "Night, night. Love you." is what her mother used to say to all of us each evening before bedtime!

I thought again about the smell of my dad's cherry tobacco years ago in my kitchen. I thought again about the ghostly image of Judy standing by her grave and saluting me. I thought again about Linda's yellow Post-it note that came floating down from a clear blue sky.

Why do I always seem to hear "Unchained Melody" when I'm sad or lonely. Why does a red cardinal come and sit on a tree branch near where I'm having my morning coffee on the deck? Why did a butterfly land gently on my hand as I was gardening one peaceful summer afternoon? These were all events where an unconscious need was met, where something happened at just the perfect time.

I was so grateful to receive these messages of love, comfort, and reassurance. The more *aware* I became of their existence, the easier it was for me to recognize them, no matter how subtle. Our soul is the larger part of us that is always aware of its connection to God. It has the broadest perspective of our life. It will always guide us if we just pay attention.

And I also thought about the importance of that sense of gratitude. I realized that routinely talking about gratitude with those whom I loved had a higher spiritual benefit of making us feel more connected to one another.

Terri and I had talked a lot about gratitude over the years. Ours was a friendship formed on the first day we had met and lasted thirty-five years. She was by my side during some of the most frightening days of my life. Our sheer perseverance had led us through a successful business that allowed each of us to get the home of our dreams. We had laughed so much that we blamed that laughter for the wrinkles on our faces. We had so much to be grateful for.

Linda and I had talked a lot about gratitude. We talked about "God-incidences." We thought there was no such thing as a coincidence because God was always giving us what we needed and when we needed it. We had started to share the preparation for our weekly Bible studies and oftentimes had deep conversations about the importance of faith and trusting in God's timing. We had so much to be grateful for.

Tom and I had talked a lot about gratitude too. From the early days of high school right up through his final days, we talked about how grateful we were to have each other. We had the kind of love that can only happen once in a lifetime. We had each faced some tough challenges, only to find each other again after so many years. We had so much to be grateful for.

Gratitude can help to sculpt you into someone who grows with deeper appreciation, who more readily recognizes opportunities, who laughs more heartily, who believes in possibilities, and most importantly, who loves more openly.

*****

I had bounced in and out of the various stages of grief. I had felt the depths of pain, and I lived there for a long time. Reflecting on the heavenly signs I had received and the depth of gratitude that I felt for having such cherished people in my life brought me to the realization that my acceptance of these deaths started with finding meaning for their lives.

Death ends a life. It does not end our relationship, our love, or our hope. Life offers us many layers of meaning, and it's our choice to decide what we are going to do with that meaning. Finding meaning changed my pain and ended my suffering.

When Mom died, I was sitting next to her bed with my hand on her leg as she took her last breath. The sadness of it all gripped my soul, and I was unprepared for such a loss.

When Dad died, I was traveling to see him at the hospital, but I didn't make it in time. I was devastated that I didn't have the chance to say goodbye.

When Tom died, I had just stepped outside with Pastor Mary when Lois yelled out to say he was gone. She was convinced that he did not want me to be there when he passed away.

When Linda died, I was traveling back from the Vietnam Veteran Ceremony that had celebrated Tom's sacrifice for his country. It had been so grueling to leave her just a couple of days before.

When Terri died, I was sitting next to her bed, holding her hand as she took her last breath, and I thought that was the most sacred moment of my life. At the time, I was surprised at that thought. Why did I feel Terri's death was sacred? I was touching my mother when she had died, just as I was touching Terri. For a long time, I could not explain why I felt that way. But now, because of my journey through grief, I finally understood.

Mom's death was the first death in our immediate family. She had been such an important, strong, and loving role model. I was truly unprepared to lose my mother. Of course, her death was sacred. Dad's death was sacred. Tom's death was sacred. Linda's death was sacred.

I felt Terri's death was sacred at that moment because I had *finally* learned, through my painful grief journey, to find meaning in death, to find meaning in grief. Loss is what happens to us in life. Meaning is what we make happen.

I felt peace slowly seep into my being. Although my steps sometimes faltered, I knew I was being tenderly guided. Through God's amazing grace, I had the ability to wade through all of the layers of meaning and to choose a new path.

*****

SIGNS, GRATITUDE, AND MEANING

Reflections

1. Do you believe in "heavenly signs?" Do you believe that our lost loved ones can communicate with us? Why or why not?

   _____
   _____
   _____
   _____

2. Gratitude enriches human life and can build a greater connection and bond between two people. Describe how you use the power of gratitude in your relationships?

   _____
   _____
   _____
   _____

3. Loss can wound and paralyze. It can hang over us for years. But finding meaning in loss empowers us to find a path forward. Do you struggle to find meaning in situations that don't make sense to you? Try to find meaning in something you are struggling with now.

   _____
   _____
   _____
   _____

CHAPTER 16

My Journey Continues...

> There are two ways of spreading light: be the
> candle or the mirror that reflects it.
> —Edith Wharton

Lisa was a friend of Linda's daughter April. I had met her several times over the years whenever I traveled to New Jersey to spend time with April. Lisa had three grown children, and she had recently remarried. She had decided to quit her job and continue her accounting business full-time from her home.

She called one day, and after a lengthy conversation, we decided she should come and visit me. That visit was a holy moment. It was a God-moment. It was a perfectly timed moment.

Two important events happened during that visit. First of all, we learned how much we had in common and how our lives had so many parallels. She had been a single mother after an unhealthy first marriage. She was an entrepreneur. She had a deep faith. She loved country music, walking, gardening, spicy foods, and jigsaw puzzles. It was eerie. The longer we talked, the more I realized how exciting it might be to have someone to share similar lessons we had each learned over the years. Perhaps we could even enjoy some of our favorite activities together.

Secondly, our conversation eventually took a more profound turn. Her husband, John, had recently been diagnosed with a rare brain disorder and had been forced to retire. Very unexpectedly, and what seemed like overnight, Lisa was suddenly his primary caregiver. Although Lisa was twenty years younger than me, it felt as though she was on the verge of living so much of what I had experienced with Tom's disease.

Our first visit quickly turned into more frequent visits. Sometimes she would stay overnight, and other times, she might stay for a few days. Sprinkled throughout our long conversations over endless hours, there was a kind of wholehearted laughter I hadn't experienced in years.

And there were hugs—*hello* hugs, *goodbye* hugs, and *spontaneous* hugs after laughing or crying. There were those *just-because* hugs. I realized that by living alone for so many years, I had become hug deprived! I had plenty of friends and acquaintances, but it was only my weekly Bible-study group that I saw on a regular basis. Michelle and her husband were wrapped up in busy work schedules and raising kids. I saw them as often as possible, but there had been no daily physical contact. And Andy and his family lived three thousand miles away. Hugs are important. They are healing, healthy, and fun. I had missed them.

Serendipity? Synchronicity? Our friendship unfolded with no conscious effort. We both continually expressed a deep sense of gratitude to God for allowing our paths to cross. This friendship, this soul connection, was not a coincidence.

I thought about those heavenly signs and messages I had witnessed over the years. And now there was something similar happening, but I called them "earthly signs."

Lisa and I were together in her backyard one morning when a small white feather floated down in front of us. We were surprised when it appeared out of nowhere, but we were even more in awe as it hovered in front of us for nearly an hour. It floated back and forth, up and down, but it never moved more than a foot or two. For several minutes at a time, it simply didn't move at all; it floated strangely in place right in front of us. Finally, Lisa slowly reached out and gently took it in her hand. We just looked at each other in utter amazement.

And then we put it in a small glass jar that remains in my kitchen as a visual reminder of a wonderful, unexplainable event we had shared.

But I wondered, could that feather have been representative of all my lost loved ones? It was so comforting!

After Tom died, my grandkids gave me *The Night Before Christmas* storybook he and I had recorded so that I could hear his voice whenever I wanted to. I wanted to share it with Lisa so that she, too, could hear his voice. As I opened the book, she said, "I've already seen this."

I said, "No, you haven't, because this is the first time I've seen it in years!"

But then she proceeded to tell me details she had no way of knowing! She knew that Tom's voice had stuttered a little on one of the verses. She knew that we had read the last page of the book together. Again, we were both stunned by another unexplainable event.

But were those events *really* unexplainable? No, we didn't think so. We thought they were undeniable earthly signs that reinforced the fact that our friendship was something uncommon, something designed as a gift from God at just the perfect time. Our lives became embedded in one another.

When my younger brother died of Lou Gehrig's disease, I had traveled back home to attend his funeral. I was to speak at his service, so I prepared some words to share about our growing up in a loving family. I wanted to talk about the important things we had in common because of our parents and how we were raised. I wanted to remind my family and all those in attendance that love is our common denominator.

As I entered the building, I knew I would struggle with the words when I looked out over the sadness in the room. But then I saw Lisa and John sitting in the front row! They had made the long trip that day just to be there with me. It was something I will never forget.

Also, I was struck by the characteristics in Lisa that reminded me of Tom, Linda, and Terri. She had Tom's selfless, caring manner as she always put the needs of others before her own. She had Linda's

MY JOURNEY CONTINUES...

deep faith and eventually joined my weekly Bible-study group, where she quickly became an inspiration to everyone. She had Terri's hopeful outlook and sense of humor, with laughter being a main ingredient in her daily life. Their memories were kept even more alive through her presence.

John was suffering from a slowly progressive disease. I told Lisa about the myriad of caregiving duties—how depression and anxiety slowly creep into your days, how worrying and witnessing declining health conditions can nearly immobilize you at times, how fatigue and sleep deprivation can hamper decision-making, how unfamiliar financial concerns can materialize with even a single new prescription, how quickly the loss of time for self-care can emerge, how daily stress can affect the best of relationships, how guilty feelings can crush an already tired heart, how grief at losing a once-vibrant life together can seep into your mind unnoticed.

I thought that perhaps if she read my manuscript for this book, she could better understand what I had gone through. After she had finished reading it, she made a startling observation. She looked at me and firmly stated, "God is not finished with you yet."

"Be positive. Be faithful. Never give up." Those words uttered by my mother as she was near death now came rushing back to me.

"Be positive. Be faithful. Never give up." These words now haunted me. I didn't have a concern with "be positive" or "be faithful," but the "never give up" left me speechless. After thinking about what Lisa had said, I realized that as I had come to terms with my losses and my grief, I had, in a very subtle way, given up. I was at peace with where I was in my life, and I was content to live with this peace until I died.

A single word popped into my head. It was *purpose*. Once again, God had placed an incredible opportunity in front of me. I could use all of the wisdom I had accumulated over the years to help Lisa through her difficult times ahead. Through Lisa, God had given me a new purpose. "God is not finished with you yet." Her words shook me to my core! What a moment!

I looked at the puzzle I was calling my life. I had almost put all the pieces together. My virtual tour had explored so many of my life's experiences. It had uncovered a barrage of feelings that helped lead me to a deeper understanding of my grief. But as comforting as this was, the puzzle was not yet complete. God wasn't finished with me yet.

*****

I've stepped back, looked at my life, and seen that it has been just as it was designed. My journey through grief had a profound purpose.

We all have a purpose in life, and fulfilling that purpose can take us through extraordinary and unexpected experiences. We will meet remarkable people along the way at different places, at different times, and for different reasons.

Fulfilling our purpose is a choice. It can be missed if we are drowning in the busyness of daily life. It can be missed if we are caught up in relationship issues. It can be missed if we are focusing only on ourselves, much like how I had allowed my life to be submerged in grief.

My thoughts turned to Tom again. Many times, I would go out to his jobsite to help him clean up and gather all his tools and equipment to put back in his truck. Whether he was building a new house or remodeling an older home, he always wrote his name and date on a board somewhere inside the structure. He told me that he did that because he simply wanted to "leave his mark" on the world. Now each time I visit his grave, I tell him what a wonderful mark he has left on this world!

Because of my journey through grief, I have experienced positive psychological changes in myself. I have a deeper appreciation for life. I want more meaningful relationships with family and friends. I have an increased sense of personal strength. I realize there are always new possibilities in life. My spiritual life has deepened. I am no longer a victim but a victor over my losses. My grief no longer controls me.

In closing, I invite you to take a virtual tour of your life. Try to eliminate asking *why* and replace your questions with *what*. See how

MY JOURNEY CONTINUES...

you have actually created your own reality by not only the choices that you have made but also by how you chose to react to each of life's major events. I invite you to open your hearts and minds and realize that circumstances cannot steal your joy without your permission.

I've learned the only way to move beyond the pain is to move through the pain. Surviving grief is not about understanding death; it's about learning how to live life after death. Moving beyond grief requires the willingness to share our healing experience with those who are still suffering. It is only by sharing ourselves that we begin to receive a portion of that which was lost.

Live your life with hope. God is not finished with you yet.

> Death is not extinguishing the light; it is only putting
> out the lamp because the dawn has come.
> —Rabindranath Tagore

ABOUT THE AUTHOR

Mary Lynn was born in Tidioute, a small town in Northwestern Pennsylvania. She was one of eight children, and upon high school graduation, she served six years in the United States Air Force during the Vietnam War era. Her duty stations included Eglin AFB in Florida and Hickam AFB in Hawaii, where she was introduced to and gained valuable experience in what was then known as the data-processing career field.

Her years in the military helped to jumpstart a successful career in the information-technology sector that spanned a period of over forty years. She retired in 2009 as chief program officer for the state of Delaware's Department of Technology and Information and then became the primary caregiver for her husband, Tom.

She currently lives in Dover, Delaware, where she has been an active volunteer since the death of her husband. She is a member of the Dover Presbyterian Church, where she served as an ordained deacon for several years. She is currently the Kent County mentor coordinator for the Superior Court Veterans Treatment Court, working with troubled veterans as they strive to find a more-productive and law-abiding life. She is also a volunteer chaplain and patient companion for the Delaware Hospice organization.

Mary Lynn's hobbies include gardening, writing, reading, traveling, and long-distance walking. She has two children and five grandchildren.